THE BLACK FLAG OF ANARCHY

THE
BLACK
FLAG
OF
ANARCHY

ANTISTATISM IN THE UNITED STATES

Corinne Jacker

Charles Scribner's Sons   •   New York

Acknowledgments

The lines on page 170 are from "Justice Denied in Massachusetts." From COLLECTED POEMS, Harper & Row. Copyright 1928, 1955 by Edna St. Vincent Millay and Norma Millay Ellis. By permission of Norma Millay Ellis.

The quotation from Ayn Rand on page 179 is from FOR THE NEW INTELLECTUAL, Random House. Copyright 1961 by Ayn Rand. By permission of Random House.

A - 3.68 [MC]

Printed in the United States of America
Library of Congress Catalog Card Number 68-12518

For Joseph H. Braun

                                    The man
Of virtuous soul commands not, nor obeys:
Power, like a desolating pestilence,
Pollutes whate'er it touches, and obedience
Bane of all genius, virtue, freedom, truth,
Makes slaves of men, and, of the human frame,
A mechanized automaton.

                              Percy Bysshe Shelley

CONTENTS

LIST OF ILLUSTRATIONS

1

What Is Anarchism?

It is commonly believed that society in a condition of anarchy—that is, without government, law, or authority—would be in complete disorder: a world where chaos would rule, where the innocent would be totally unprotected from robbery and murder, where the strongest would have everything and the weak nothing, where morality would disappear and where "anything goes."

This is a fairly cynical viewpoint. It implies that if human beings were left to their own devices they would be so depraved, so lacking in morality that they would quickly revert to a near-animal state where the only thing that mattered would be one's own satisfaction.

Anarchists have a more romantic approach to life. They believe in the perfectibility of mankind and that, left to himself and properly educated, man would voluntarily act in an ethical and socially beneficial way. Anarchists are convinced that the individual must be completely free; there must be no authority to dictate his behavior or its limits. Each person should govern himself. If men want to get together, they believe, the society they form should be established by mutual consent and anyone should be able to withdraw from it whenever he feels it is in his best interests to do so.

The anarchist rejects any rule and any person or institution that endeavors to enforce it, because rules are an attempt to restrict an individual's freedom. He must also then reject government and the laws that governments make, as well as the police whose job is to enforce laws; for him no government, no matter how liberal it may be, or how democratic its institutions are, is acceptable.

Since one way to define the State is as the embodiment of government and law, the anarchist is convinced that it must disappear in order to make men truly free; in fact, another term for anarchism is *antistatism*. Defined in this way, there is a clear distinction between *society,* which is composed of the individuals who voluntarily and freely comprise it, and the *State,* an artificially structured community that oppresses men through its authority to limit their behavior in accordance with certain laws and customs.

Phrased another way, the anarchist sets up natural man, who is totally free in his behavior, as the ideal man; in opposition to natural man as the civilized individual, bound by political behavior that involves paying taxes, serving in the army, supporting public schools, and all the other actions required of him by his government.

As the population of the world continues to grow and cities become more crowded, there is a growing tendency to increase the authority of police, and the state or federal government needs more clerks and electronic computers to keep track of the records each person accumulates. This is the only way to control antisocial behavior.

On the other hand, a town of two or three hundred inhabitants can readily exist without a police force and even without a mayor and specially elected town council. When decisions have to be made, the whole community can make them together, whether it be a question of adding fluoride to the drinking water, changing the course of instruction at the local high school, or building a new town monument—the man who lives in New York or Chicago has no direct say in any of these matters. For this reason, in anarchist writings there is an urge toward decentralization, a desire to get back to small communities operating independently and so structured that they are self-supporting, each community making its own products, growing its own food, and doctoring its own sick.

In the same way, when a few men decide they will weave fabrics, saw lumber, or make shoes, regulation of their work is not necessary. But conditions are quite different in a factory where thousands of workers are employed and where the products— cars, jet planes, or television sets—are so complicated that only one or two men understand the whole process. Rules must be made for the protection of both owner and employee. Working hours have to be regulated, minimum wages set, performance standards established, and work loads defined. In his opposition to authority, the anarchist necessarily finds himself against modern urban industrial society; he has been hopelessly defeated by the changes technology and science have made in civilization.

In essence, then, the anarchist believes in the free, unhampered life for an individual who governs himself in all his actions without being restricted in any way by authority. Any person may voluntarily join with other free individuals in societies that operate with no external government but by mutual, voluntary agreement. In order to believe that such a society is possible, the anarchist has to be an idealist. He has to be convinced that man is basically altruistic, that it is eventually possible to establish utopian societies, paradises on earth where men live peacefully together.

Antistatists find some justification for this point of view in the thinking of the nineteenth-century German philosopher Georg W. F. Hegel, who believed that the history of the world is one of progress in the consciousness of freedom. Further support comes from Charles Darwin, who developed the idea that man, like all other organisms, evolved from early primeval microorganisms to the complicated animal he is now. For the anarchist, mutual aid and freedom are evolutionary advances; he believes that society is evolving to an anarchistic condition that is its highest form.

There are several other points on which all anarchists are agreed. First, those who try to enforce man-made laws upon a naturally evolving free society are its real enemies. No matter what degree of violence an anarchist may advocate, he is not antisocial but trying rather to help society back onto what he believes is the natural road to human liberty and happiness. Second, social and moral evils such as poverty, robbery, prostitution, and discrimination cannot be cured by the State, which actually is the servant of the oppression and exploitation that cause these evils. Third, all reforms beginning from above (that is, from the authority of government) are worthless. Only changes that begin locally and gradually expand to a federal and then international level can be successful.

From these points comes the fourth area of agreement: The only way to have a new society based on individual freedom is to destroy the State; depending on the type of antistatism involved, this destruction should be either violent and sudden or slow and through education. This destruction is necessary, the antistatist believes, because civilization as it now exists is a series of obstacles that prevents man from fulfilling his human potential. A kind of asceticism is inherent in this criticism of urban, technological society; the anarchist wants to get rid of all superfluous material objects and services. What is left, the human needs for food, shelter, and companionship can then, within the natural laws of society, be satisfied.

Several types of anti-authoritarianism exist. The first conscious anarchism was the sort known as mutualism. It began with the work of the poet Shelley's father-in-law William Godwin (1756–

WILLIAM GODWIN

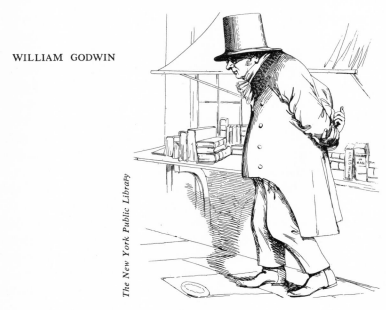

The New York Public Library

• 4 •

1836). His book, *Enquiry Concerning Political Justice,* published in 1793 under the pseudonym Edward Baldwin, was the first formulation of a political and economic philosophy of anarchism. Godwin's work was followed by that of the Frenchman Pierre Joseph Proudhon, whose major statement was in his 1840 work *What is Property?* The proponents of mutualism assumed that the basis for all human societies was the contract, a reasonable, voluntary agreement between men. These antistatists thought that the State should give way to small communes and workers' cooperaitves, which would form larger federations in time. There were to be contracts of exchange and mutual credit among the individuals in one group as well as among all the communities. While the economic and social ideas of mutualism were soon out of date because of the rapidly changing society of the nineteenth century, the philosophy of the mutualists helped to shape more advanced forms of antistatism.

Religious, or Christian, anarchism found its most famous speaker in the great Russian writer Leo Tolstoy, and it is sometimes called Tolstoyism. Yet he, like many others, identified the word *anarchism* with violence and armed rebellion and so refused to allow himself to be called an anarchist. Nevertheless, his opposition to the State and to all authority put him in the anti-authoritarian camp.

Religious anarchism is almost always associated with pacifism, that is, nonviolence, and refusal to participate in wars or to bear arms. For religious anarchists, the ideal community is a small, essentially agricultural, voluntary society. They have been confronted with a problem no other radical thinkers have had to face: once pacifist anarchists recognized what they considered to be the brutalities and injustices of the State, they had to find ways to fight it that were compatible with their religious principles.

Since the objection was essentially against the State or its instruments—police, law courts, members of the civil service— the only way to protest was through acts of civil disobedience; but because these individuals were deeply religious and committed to nonviolence, the disobedience had to be peaceable in nature: riot, mob violence, or assassination were unacceptable. Instead,

Tolstoy, and later the Indian leader Mohandas Gandhi, formulated the concept of passive nonresistance. This is not a negative act: while the man who chooses not to obey some law in order to make his social or political point does not make any positive threat or act of aggression against the State or its representatives, he does choose to disobey it, despite the consequences.

In a sit-in, for example, the demonstrators simply sit in restaurants or public places where a law or custom, which they consider to be unjust, forbids it. If police or others with authority order the demonstrators to move, they usually refuse to do so. The only possible nonviolent resistance to forcible eviction is passive —just to sit or lie limply and force the police or other officials to carry one out. As the British found in India, massive nonresistance can paralyze a country. Moreover, the government is put in the embarrassing situation of having to arrest and punish peaceful citizens who do not resist, who have committed no violent acts at all. In the eyes of the rest of society, this makes the State seem the aggressor anarchists think it is.

Because they believe in divine power and in the Kingdom of God, all religious anarchists derive their philosophical justification from a conviction that the State is a profanation of God's will. To them it expresses man's sinful pride when he tries to take the Lord's place as ethical authority and lawgiver. The only law is moral law made by God.

In the United States during World War I, pacifist anarchists were actively trying to convince young men of military age to refuse to serve in the armed forces. They were against Liberty Bonds, war taxes, and any other direct or indirect support of the war. In this effort they were joined by immigrant anarchists but not by the other native antistatists. Dorothy Day and Ammon Hennacy, two of the most famous American religious anarchists, were active in the pacifist movement. Hennacy, in fact, served two years in solitary confinement because of his antiwar activities. To Hennacy, the Kingdom of God was in everyone. He wrote: "The only revolution worthwhile was the one-man revolution within the heart. Each one could make this by himself and need not wait on a majority."

During the depression, in 1933, Miss Day founded the *Catholic Worker*, a newspaper that became a significant voice of Christian anarchism. She also tried to establish "houses of hospitality" to help workers who could find no jobs, the idea being that in these houses they could help one another by the principle of mutual aid. The movement was called the "Green Revolution," the color green being chosen because it represented hope. Beyond mutual aid, the program included ownership by the workers of the means of production, abolition of the assembly line and highly specialized labor, decentralized factories, and the restoration of hand crafts and individual ownership of property and production. The anarchists in the Green Revolution, like many Christian saints and preachers, voluntarily accepted poverty as a part of their existence. Their goals, however, were incompatible with the rapidly increasing industrialization of the United States and the Western world in general.

It would not have been possible—barring some catastrophic natural disaster or a great miracle—to make society revert to the agrarian, nontechnological world of the past. While the *Catholic Worker* still exists and Miss Day remains a noted and respected commentator on society, the larger social changes the American Christian anarchists believed in are no longer considered feasible. However, their creed of nonviolence and pacifism has greatly affected other libertarian movements, particularly the civil rights movement of the 1950's and 60's and the current antiwar demonstrations.

The most successful and well-known type of anarchism in Europe is known as collectivist anarchism or anarcho-communism. Its originators were the Italian Enrico Malatesta and the Russians Mikhail Bakunin and Peter Kropotkin. These philosophers derived their viewpoint from Godwin, Proudhon, and the mutualists, but they varied the way in which a worker would enjoy the product of his labor. While he would still be given goods and services equal to what he produced, the worker would have no individual, or private, property. Instead, the voluntary small organizations of workers, known as collectives, would have ownership of every material object. Each person would be given his food, clothing, furniture, and all other substance from a common stock: from each according to his means, to each according to his need.

Underlying Bakunin's and Kropotkin's ideas of social structure was a rebellion against the rapid industrialization of the nineteenth century—something they, like all the other anarchist thinkers, could not accept. Not only did the increasing specialization seem to be dehumanizing the workers, but the rapid growth of cities around centers of manufacture was breeding slums where workers lived in unsanitary and crowded conditions. Labor was being increasingly exploited by owners of mills and factories. Against all this, Bakunin set up as his ideal society communes based on the Russian peasant villages; Kropotkin's model was the small village of the Middle Ages.

Collectivist anarchists had little hope that the owners of large capitalistic enterprises or the heads of government benefiting from these industries would ever want to reform the very conditions that were promoting their wealth and power. Instead, they sought the founders of collectivism in the peasant, who was still uncorrupted by the perverting and debilitating influences of the technological society. That peasants did not respond in great numbers to the call of anarchism seemed only to be proof that the only way to success was in complete withdrawal from the State. Because of its emphasis on agricultural collectivism, communist anarchism was most popular in the least industrialized southern countries—Italy, Spain, and France.

Kropotkin, who was convinced that anarchism was a natural evolutionary tendency of society, believed that communism and anarchism were mutually complementary aspects of evolution and that one needed the other to succeed. He could find ample support for this idea in the writings of Marx and Engels, the first communist theorists. In communist theory, at the most advanced stages of socialist society, economic exploitation of the worker would no longer exist, and he would be free to act in ways that accorded with his own interest, which by definition would also be in the interest of the group. Once this happened, it would be unnecessary to continue the oppressive controls of

PRINCE PETER KROPOTKIN

Culver Pictures Inc.

government and the State would "wither away." Individuals would voluntarily perform actions that had before been done only under coercion.

Lenin, the first head of the Russian State after the Revolution of 1917, also wrote on this subject. He stated that the withering away of the State would occur in the second stage of socialism, after the classes opposed to the socialist State had been destroyed and the private ownership of property had been abolished. Then, "the narrow horizons of bourgeois law" would be left behind. There would no longer even be a need for the police, because most crime was caused by want and when it disappeared crime would disappear as well. Any individual case of antisocial behavior would be handled by the "armed nation" just as men break up a fight or protect their women from assault.

Another, necessary correlate of communism that the collectivist anarchists shared was the concept that revolution is the only possible way of achieving a different, and to the communist a better, social order. Communists did not find in the *Communist Manifesto* a plea for revolution, for they were already convinced it was necessary. They found, rather, a prediction about the way revolution would happen and a guide for communists to use in order to bring it about.

Although Kropotkin refused to accept that violence was necessary, later proponents of his thought endorsed it when it was a necessary part of the class struggle or when it would be "educational." The gratuitous act of violence that was supposed to call attention to the plight of the working class, the evils of capitalism, or some other social ill was known as *propaganda by deed*. This action usually took the form of the bombing of a capitalist's home or factory, or the assassination of a government official or head of industry.

Anarcho-communism was brought to the United States in the latter half of the nineteenth century by immigrants, particularly those from Italy, Russia, and Germany. It never received strong support from native American thinkers. Yet through its leading exponents—Emma Goldman, Alexander Berkman, and Johann Most, it had an indelible effect on political and social thought in this country, especially in the painful and violent struggle of the labor unions to assert themselves.

Closely related to this type of antistatism is anarcho-syndicalism, which was advocated by radical trade unions in the early years of this century. The proletariat was to rise and to seize for itself all positive State functions. The weapon of the workers was the strike, through which they would shape the economic upheavals to come. Instead of the State there would arise the direct, voluntary association of the wage-earning class.

The most recent form of anarchism to develop, individualist anarchism, was found almost exclusively in the United States, and it will be the primary concern of this book. As the name implies, these antistatists were concerned with the freedom of the individual, who would live with other free persons in a voluntary nongovernment association, which would be formed through individual self-interest for economic and social convenience.

That any anarchistic movement was conceivable in the United

States raises the question of what the similarities and differences are between anarchism and democracy. Both political philosophies are opposed to oppressive government and the exploitation of the masses by a ruling class. The democrat, however, advances the concept of the sovereignty of the *people*. To the anarchist, the sovereignty of the *person* is most important.

In a democracy a government of the people, of the majority of the residents of the State, exists. In anarchy no government exists. The anarchist will never accept any kind of parliamentary organization, no matter how liberal and enlightened the government may be; this is because, under any State system for the safety and well-being of the majority, the individual must give up some of his rights. Even voting as a recognition of the authority of the State must disappear. The majority's ability to dictate behavior to the minority, no matter how small or peculiar the minority may be and how enlightened the majority may be is coming into question in recent years in America. Not only in the civil rights struggle, but in rulings on obscene literature and in the decision to eliminate prayers from public schools, the Supreme Court is apparently asserting the rights of a minority in a democratic State. The commonly accepted rule of thumb, that a minority must be controlled only when it infringes on the rights of the majority, still seems viable. Yet, the anarchist must always reject the most careful and socially perceptive legislation or jurisdiction. As William Godwin said, to him "there is but one power to which I can yield a heart-felt obedience, the decision of my own understanding, the dictate of my own conscience."[1]

2

The Origins of Anarchist Philosophy

Along with the other modern revolutionary movements, socialism and communism, anarchism is a comparatively recent political philosophy, but its roots can be traced far back in time. From the age of Classical Greece in the fifth century B.C., there have been dissenters, frequently accused of extreme pessimism and cynicism, who have argued that certain, if not all, social or religious institutions are cruel and evil. Any regulation of man's free actions, they have argued as do the anarchists, leads only to a stunting of his natural tendency toward perfectibility. With proper education and absolute freedom, men would be able to fulfill the innate potentiality for goodness, moral behavior, and intellectual growth with which they are universally endowed. Evil and ignorance, to these dissenters, are the product of repression by the State.

Many anarchists have felt that it is important to trace the historical evolution of antistatism. This dependence on a long-term background comes not from a need for support but rather because a past is essential if anarchism is what its proponents claim it to be. If the struggle against authority is taken to be a manifestation of natural urges that will become increasingly apparent throughout history, it, of course, cannot be a modern development. Further, to the antistatist "nature" is an essence and social structure as it exists an "accident," so nature must demand that men continually assert their need for freedom from law and government of all kinds.

Kropotkin's history of anarchism began with the anonymous masses of prehistoric people. He found two tendencies throughout human existence. On the one hand there was mutual aid, expressed in prehistoric tribal customs, the structure of primitive villages, and, much later, the development of the medieval craft guilds. Opposed to this was the authoritarian element in society. This started with the early shamans, village magicians, and priests, who called upon mystical authority and depended on superstition and fear to set up rigid legal and social structures of class hierarchy and taboo. Kropotkin's history of authoritarians was brought up to date by including modern lawmakers and military leaders who he believed had inherited the early oppressive tradition.

Almost any philosopher can be cited as an historical confirmation of the persistence of the basic beliefs of anarchism. A faith in the decency of mankind, the desire for individual freedom, an unwillingness to accept domination—all of these are found in classical Greek thought. But more specifically Zeno (336–264 B.C.), the founder of Stoicism, and Aristippus (fl. 430 B.C.) are usually considered to be the earliest forerunners of anarchist thought.

Aristippus began the Cyrenaic school, named after his birthplace, Cyrene, the capital of a Greek colony in northern Africa. When he was a young man, Aristippus came to Athens and became a pupil of Socrates. To the young student, pleasure was the basic goal of humanity. In response to a question from his teacher he said that he wished to be a member of neither the governed nor the governing class. He later thought that the wise should not give up any of their liberty to the State.

Zeno was more explicit in his thought and was the first to anticipate anarcho-communism. He opposed his idea of a free, governmentless community to Plato's Utopian State. Zeno believed that the State must not be omnipotent, nor should it be allowed to interfere in or regiment individual life. Instead, the moral law of the individual should rule society.

For him there were two rival instincts in human beings. First, the instinct for self-preservation, which leads to egoism. Second, the need to join with other men in a cooperative society and to behave in accord with the common good. So, if men allowed themselves to follow both impulses, they would live in peace and there would be no need for law courts, police, armies, or temples.

Even money would be unnecessary. In this stateless society, "perfect equality and freedom would restore the original good tendencies of human nature and establish universal harmony."[1] National frontiers would break down, giving way to a Cosmos— a stateless, egalitarian society where free men would be able to attain fully the possibilities within human nature.

The next major manifestation of antistatist thought occurred many centuries later in a religious environment at a time of economic revolution. Until the fourteenth century, economic and social life had remained inseparable. There was no concept in any way related to "making a living," because work was man's way of life. However, a system of commercial trade was slowly established; it was based on the three fundamental elements of economic theory: labor, land, and capital. Until about the 1300's the idea of salable or rentable land did not exist. Estates or manors were the property of noble families who also owned the labor of the serfs on the estate. Once the laborer moved from place to place and became a valuable, contracting agent in his own right, and capital was used to buy goods not to satisfy immediate needs but for the purpose of speculation and profit, the economic life of an individual was no longer identical with his social one.

Several early Christian movements, including the Hussites and the Anabaptists, stressed the moral necessities of religion and held views similar to Zeno's about the State. In the thirteenth century, the Brothers and Sisters of the Free Spirit denied the justification of all State and Church institutions and affirmed that the individual was free from the restrictions of any laws. This set the pattern of medieval antistatist thought within the Church.

Peter of Chelcic, a younger contemporary of Jan Huss, preached equality and a kind of communism that was to be realized outside the boundaries of the State. He found reason for this in his assertion that the State was evil, that it performed the work of the Devil by creating inequalities of property, rank, and place.

Antagonism between those with property and authority and those who have neither is often a source of anarchist sentiments.

This was clearly expressed in a speech by John Ball, who was sometimes called the "mad priest of Kent." Ball quarreled with the Archbishop of Canterbury, was excommunicated from the Church, and, during the Peasants' Revolt in England in 1381, urged that the mobs attack lords and lawyers. He was executed by order of Richard II in that year.

In his speech Ball said, "Things cannot go well in England, nor ever will, until all goods are held in common, and until there will be neither serfs nor gentlemen, and we shall be equal. For what reason have they, whom we call lords, got the best of us? How did they deserve it? Why do they keep us in bondage? If we all descended from one father and one mother, Adam and Eve, how can they assert or prove that they are more masters than ourselves? Except perhaps that they make us work and produce for them to spend."[2]

This confusion, resentment, and righteous disgust at the sight of injustices obviously created not by God but by man is the core of anarchists' moral stand. Ball speaks for all the men and women of his viewpoint. His inability or unwillingness to accept the evils imposed on him and his peers by a few wealthy and privileged men was magnified by those who followed him.

In later centuries an increased discontent with poverty, with the advantages taken by the ruling class, and with an ever more restricted life led to a general revolutionary trend. Men no longer believed that the state in which they were born was the one in which they would have to die. The individual consequently took an increasingly important place in men's thought. The extensive development of autobiography and biography in the sixteenth century and the rapid popularity of the novel once it was introduced as an art form indicate a general preoccupation with the emotions and psychology of individuals. Moreover, the Renaissance had again revived a belief in the perfectibility of man.

Significantly for America, which in the beginning was settled primarily by the English, the first anarchistic attempt at direct action took place in England at the end of the Civil War of 1642–49. Gerrard Winstanley, a clergyman, wrote a book called *Truth Lifting up Its Head above Scandals*, published in 1649. In it he stated that Christ was "the universal liberty," that authority corrupts; by authority, Winstanley meant all forms of power, including the domestic authority of a husband over his wife or of a father over his son. All men were entitled to equal liberty, he said. Private property, because it was a kind of authority, was evil. The only way to get justice and equality was for the people to rise up and seize the land. Winstanley was not advocating actual revolution, however, for the land he wanted the people to seize was only the waste territory that was not a part of any lord's estate nor under cultivation of any kind. In April of 1649, Winstanley and thirty or forty followers took over some vacant land. This action was construed as dangerous civil disobedience, and, opposed by neighbors and the king's troops, the group surrendered in 1650.

The English dissenters who settled in the New England colonies brought with them a sense of possible freedom derived from the sectarianism and civil rebellion of their native country. They also brought a Calvinist ethic that strongly affected American political philosophy. To the Puritans the State was a depraved institution. And a sense of economic equality, or fair proportion, among the first settlers was remarkably strong.

For example, in the town records of Lancaster, Massachusetts, the following was entered in 1653:

And whereas lots are now laid out for the most part equally to rich and poor, partly to keep the town from scattering too far, and partly out of charity and respect to men of meaner estate, yet that equality (which is the rule of God) may be observed, we covenant and agree that, in a second division and so through all other divisions of land the matter shall be drawn as near to equality according to man's estates as we are able to do. That he which hath now more than his estate deserveth in home lots and interval lots shall have so much less; and he that hath less than his estate deserveth shall have so much more.[3]

While a man's proper amount of land was based on a still strong caste system, this document is remarkably liberal for its time.

3

Colonial Roots of American Anarchism

While the Founding Fathers of the New England colonies were opposed to government in accordance with their Calvinist teachings, they regarded it as a necessary evil. And certainly they were not hesitant to work in league with the devil in this realm. The most rigorous laws were established to regulate individual behavior in the smallest areas of social, moral, and economic life, and enforcement of all the statutes was harsh. For example, blasphemy was punishable by death in the 1650 Connecticut code of laws, as was a son's outrageous unfilial behavior. As early as 1649, the good citizens of Massachusetts thought it necessary to form an association to stop the worldly luxury of long male hair.

The Massachusetts Commonwealth became the first authoritarian state in the colonies. The peril presented by hostile Indians along with the sparsely settled land without any central point of control was impossible; it made the colony's leaders, who already were impressed with their own power, even more eager to restrict the colonists. Moreover, the Royal Charter establishing the Massachusetts Bay Company was granted only on condition that the men and women living in the territory conduct their lives in a peaceful and orderly way. Heresy, disagreement with the crown's policies, or open rebellion were grounds for revocation of the charter, granted in 1629.

Thus was established a society that on the one hand believed in the evils of government, yet on the other punished its citizens viciously for any infractions of the law. In the new atmosphere of America, however, a sense of custom and habit was not yet established, and a number of persons wished to assert their right to think and act as they personally deemed proper. By 1636 the battle lines were drawn between the establishment and the rebels.

Against those dissenters from authority whom chastisement could not cure, there was one fatal way to prevent the infection of society: banishment. One of the most notable early rebels to be banished from Massachusetts was Roger Williams, who, for his refusal to conform, was ejected along with other dissenters from the colony in 1635. Williams and his friends traveled south and founded the more liberal colony of Rhode Island.

The greatest danger to the insular security of the Puritan community, however, was created by a number of new arrivals from England shortly after the basic governmental and religious structure of the colony had been established. These immigrants, dissatisfied with the corruption and oppression of their native country, had booked passage to the New World in the certainty that they would find a land of perfect freedom. Upon arrival in Boston, however, the new settlers were subjected to an examination on their beliefs much like modern immigration checks to exclude extreme radicals from this country. Whether or not the person passed the examination determined his eligibility for admission to the Church. And only members of the Church were franchised citizens of the colony. Some of the immigrants—in particular Mrs. Anne Hutchinson, Henry Vane, and John Wheelwright, all of whom settled in Boston or its vicinity—found the ministers cold and uninspired, the laws and rulings of judges arbitrary, and the community restrictive. When they attempted to assert their ideas, they received strong opposition from the community.

Mrs. Hutchinson was thirty-four or thirty-five when she and her husband followed their minister, John Cotton, to America in 1634. It is said that William Hutchinson was an unwilling member of the ship's company, there only because he was used to obeying his wife. Even the governor of the colony, John Winthrop, commented on William's weakness, calling him "a man of very mild temper and weak parts, and wholly guided by his wife." That Anne was a confident, strong-willed woman used to getting her own way is attested to by another member of the community, Cotton Mather; he described her as "a gentlewoman of an haughty carriage, busy spirit, competent wit and a voluble tongue."[1] Goody Hutchinson had a different kind of reputation among the women. To them she was known as a sympathetic and skilled midwife and a good and loyal friend.

As Anne Hutchinson settled down to life in Boston, it became usual for a select circle of her friends to gather at her home regularly. She would give the assembled company summaries of the sermons she had heard in church on Sunday and Thursday of the preceding week. Soon these summaries became only topics to stimulate her own speeches on ideas that she found interesting. These ideas often differed from those expressed during the church services by the minister, John Wilson. She, a woman, was setting herself up as a minister of the gospel and in effect claiming that her authority to interpret biblical text and religious doctrine was equal to or greater than Wilson's.

Anne Hutchinson was a popular speaker. Within a short time as many as sixty persons came to these informal meetings to hear her talk. Governor Winthrop soon saw in this woman and her followers a threat to his authority and to the whole basis upon which the colony was founded. It was easy to suspect her of witchcraft, because, as Mather said, "It was wonderful to see with what a speedy and spreading fascination these doctrines did bewitch the minds of people, which one would not have imagined being so besotted."[2]

The differences between this group of dissenters and the organized Church grew more pronounced, and they eventually established their own sect, becoming known as Antinomians. The very name of the sect, derived from the Greek meaning "against the law," is an indication of the anarchistic nature of their thinking, an enormous difference from the Calvinism of the Massachusetts ministers.

The Antinomians believed that the "Elect" were a chosen group of the faithful who were above a man-made, rigid, and rather petty moral code. They opposed the narrow dogmatism and formalism of the Church. Instead of this, the Elect could be guided in their actions by their own inner sense of morality and religion, which would indicate the correct way to a good life. Thus, for the Elect—which included Anne Hutchinson and her followers—laws were not only unnecessary formal codifications of truths that were already known instinctively, but they could damage and destroy the free spirit of the Elect. This is, of course, a statement of Christian anarchism almost identical to that mentioned earlier. It falls short of a full commitment to the antistatist position because the Elect were the only ones above the law and, obviously, all of society did not compose the Elect.

In 1635 the young, adventurous Henry Vane came to Massachusetts and soon became a member of the Hutchinson group. Vane had a direct and warm personality that almost immediately attracted people to him. His interests, however, were more political than religious, and he soon became active in the political life of the colony. Within a few months it was evident that this young ally of the Antinomians was yet a further threat to Winthrop's power.

The next year, both the Antinomians and Vane were at the height of their powers, and Vane was elected Governor of the colony. Anne's brother-in-law, the Reverend John Wheelwright, emigrated to Massachusetts. An attempt was made to have Wheelwright appointed assistant to the Reverends Wilson and Cotton, but since his agreement with his sister-in-law's beliefs was apparent, the position was denied him. In answer to the rebuff, Wheelwright left Boston and established his own church. He began openly to preach the Antinomian doctrine.

On January 19, 1637, Wheelwright delivered a sermon in opposition to religious fasts, arguing that they should not be observed. This open flouting of established custom and doctrine in the colony was inflammatory and had a great effect on both the Antinomians and the more conservative members of the community. In fact, Wheelwright had opposed fasting less for religious reasons than that it had been made a law. Although it was clear that the Elect, the true Christians, were undoubtedly few in number, it was also apparent that in this sermon Wheelwright was inciting them to open rebellion against the State and to the establishment of a Christian-anarchist society.

The situation was now at an impasse. The Antinomians had

openly challenged the right of authority in the colony. Winthrop had to crush them if he was to maintain his power and the established social and religious structure. On March 9, Wheelwright was called before the Assembly and accused of advocating violence against the magistrates and ministers of the colony. He was found guilty of sedition and contempt of court; the sentence was disenfranchisement and banishment.

The Antinomians and their sympathizers answered with a petition protesting the conviction. Beyond those who signed the protest, there was a larger number of citizens dissatisfied with this arbitrary action by Winthrop. The government was still in danger. It was openly attacked on another front when Vane decided to run again for governor in the next election. In August of 1637 the election was held and Winthrop was returned to office. Disgusted at the narrow-mindedness of the colonists and angry at his failure, Vane sailed for England, leaving America permanently.

Once their chief political and religious support was eliminated, it was much easier for the colony's founders to find ways to rid themselves completely of the threat of heresy and rebellion. At the end of August, a synod met at what is now Cambridge and drew up a list of beliefs that would be considered heretical. The group also passed a resolution stating that Anne Hutchinson and the other Antinomians were guilty of disorderly conduct.

Finally, on November 7, 1637, Anne was ordered to appear in Cambridge. She was questioned extensively for two days without being allowed counsel. Like the later trials for witchcraft, these court proceedings were a mockery. She was insulted by the officers of the court and forced to give evidence against herself. The verdict, no surprise to anyone, was guilty. Although Anne was pregnant, no leniency was shown to her. The sentence of banishment was carried out, and she and her main supporters were disenfranchised and evicted from the colony. Anne Hutchinson was killed in the late summer of 1643 by a band of marauding Indians.

Soon after their banishment, in 1638, the Antinomians settled on the island of Aquidneck in Rhode Island. There is some indication that they, or at least some of their number, continued to practice their doctrine and did without benefit of the judiciary or any formal laws.

This small band of dissenters and their fate mark an important point in American history. The Antinomians were the first immigrants to the New World to openly announce their disillusionment with the American way of life. Moreover, the assertion of the individual's right to rebel against authority marked an emphasis on individual liberty that was to become basic to the United States' political structure. Another precedent was set. Afraid that future immigrants would infect the members of the Massachusetts colony with new heresies or more dangerous political theories, the Massachusetts authorities in 1637 passed the first Alien Act in American history. By the terms of this act, no one was allowed to immigrate to Massachusetts "who might be dangerous to the Commonwealth." Since the Antinomians had already been declared dangerous, any friends of the Hutchinsons or sympathizers with their beliefs were barred from settling in the colony. If they did arrive, they were given four months to make other plans and then forced to leave.

Since 1637 a number of other acts have attempted to limit immigration to this country in various ways. The act of 1903, for example, excluded professed anarchists from the United States. In the early years, however, no amount of restriction could stop the influx of men and women in search of the ideal society of their dreams.

That the individual would soon dominate American political thought and that governments should tremble before his power was foreshadowed in the works of Roger Williams, one of the most noted political philosophers of his age. Williams was certainly not an anarchist, but his insistence on the rights of the individual and his denial of the divine right of government laid the groundwork for the philosophy both of the leaders of the American Revolution and of the founders of native American anarchism. Williams first asserted a distinction between the State and government. The State was organized society, and the government was the functioning action of the State. Both rested upon the *voluntary* consent of the citizens; and no form of government had a "divine right" to exist. The State's function was to supply the individual with as much freedom and economic security as possible. Williams regarded Rhode Island as a great experiment in democracy, to be founded, he wrote in his "Letter to the Town of Providence," on strict "liberty and equality, both in land and government."

Men were increasingly interested in asserting their individual rights. Monarchy was no longer a totally satisfactory form of the State; nor should Church and State be one and the same unit. The libertarian spirit in the American colonies grew rapidly. It was aided by a new political theory becoming popular in England in the last years of the seventeenth century: this was the concept that the individual was perhaps more important than the State, or, in a different phraseology, a State is based upon private property and exists primarily to protect that property. This point of view certainly appealed to the Yankee middle-class merchants who were spreading throughout the New England colonies.

That the governor and his staff were really the servants of the governed was an appealing idea; if it were so, any form of authority could be questioned and regarded as unsatisfactory. After Williams promulgated his ideas, the citizens of the Massachusetts Commonwealth were less willing to unquestioningly accept authority, as Joseph Dudley found out. Dudley was made royal governor of the colony in 1702. Three years later, in the winter of 1705, he was driving his carriage along a snowy road lined on each side with high drifts. Dudley was stopped by two carters who were coming toward him with loads of firewood. The governor ordered the men out of his way. They eyed the snowdrifts and their cargo and then refused, one saying, "I am as good flesh and blood as you. . . . You may go out of the way." The argument became more heated, but the carters remained adamant. Governor Dudley finally had the two men arrested, but they were later set free. The common man in America was no longer willing, as Dudley wrote his superiors in England, to "in the Governor's sight pull off their hats."[3]

Emigrants to America in the 1700's came less for religious freedom than for economic opportunity. From England, Scotland, Ireland, and Germany they came. In Europe they were peasants, involuntarily idle and inescapably poor; in the New World they were transformed into freeholders who by toil and luck could reach economic independence and perhaps even wealth.

Like every wave of immigrants, this group brought new ideas with them. The Enlightenment was spreading throughout England and the Continent; this was the Age of Reason. Among this philosophy's major beliefs were a trust in the natural goodness of man, his ability to be improved, and above all the belief that through the rational mind all things were possible, including the casting of society into a better mold.

One immigrant, a French gentleman, Hector St. John de Crèvecoeur, arrived in the colonies in 1759 or 1760 and wrote about what it was like suddenly to be in a new world in his *Letters from an American Farmer*:

> An European when he first arrives seems limited in his intentions, as well as in his views; but he very suddenly alters his scale . . . he no sooner breathes our air than he forms new schemes, and embarks in designs he never would have thought of in his own country. . . .
>
> He begins to feel the effects of a sort of resurrection; hitherto he had not lived, but simply vegetated; he now feels himself a man, because he is treated as such; the laws of his own country had overlooked him in his insignificancy; the laws of this cover him with their mantle.[4]

The writers of Europe were seriously conjecturing about the establishment of a Utopia, a perfect society; it was possible that the New World would be such a community. The settlers found not only human dignity in America; for the first time in their lives they came upon apparently endless miles of land that belonged to no one and could be theirs for the taking. Beyond each settlement was more uninhabited land to explore; this was the frontier, the major factor in the shaping of American destiny. When Crèvecoeur came it may have been only the wilds of Connecticut and North Carolina, but because it was there a man might make his own destiny in his own way. Of it Crèvecoeur wrote:

Near the last inhabited districts . . . men seem to be placed . . . beyond the reach of government, which in some measure leaves them to themselves . . . . The few magistrates they have are in general little better than the rest; they are often in a perfect state of war; that of man against man, sometimes decided by blows, sometimes by means of law . . . men are wholly left dependent upon their native tempers, and on the spur of uncertain industry, which often fails when not sanctified by the efficacy of a few moral rules. There, remote from the power of example, and check of shame, many families exhibit the most hideous parts of our society.[5]

The complexities and niceties of town and urban life were destroyed by the wilderness of the frontier. The only form of social organization possible was based loosely on the family. The frontiersman found himself on his own against nature, Indians, and, sometimes other settlers. Conditions tended to make him antisocial, and this was reinforced by the fact that, aside from trips to some town for provisions, a pioneer family might go months without seeing any other settlers. The pioneer could not feel that he was under the control of state or federal authorities. He tended to resist compulsory taxes and local law officials who tried to enforce regulations made hundreds of miles away or across the ocean. Under these conditions, individual liberty was often confused with the absence of all effective government. The men who were imbued with this spirit had little respect for or identification with the English crown and were readily persuaded to rebel against it. Though it lent itself to the development of democracy, the essence of the frontier can only be called anarchistic.

The pioneer seldom had time to be altruistic. He was alone in his war with the land and the Indians. Alexis de Tocqueville, another keen observer from France, wrote, "It was realized that in order to clear this land, nothing less than the constant and self-interested efforts of the owner himself was essential; the ground prepared, it became evident that its produce was not sufficient to enrich at the same time both an owner and a farmer. The land was then broken up into small portions, which the proprietor cultivated for himself."[6] This self-interest, a kind of egoism, motivated these men more than any national or territorial ties could. When pioneers were willing to band together, they did so only for companionship, safety, and mutual aid.

Their society was a paradigm of the anarchist community. In the voluntary, mutual-aid communities or alone, the pioneer no longer followed the traditional patterns of law and government. Social institutions, too, were destroyed. The tailor, the shoemaker, any specialized artisan found it hard to live by the one craft alone. The formal customs and artificial politeness of the Eastern town simply could not exist when men lived miles from one another in crude log shacks and spent most of their waking hours working. The frontiersman was increasingly unwilling to allow anyone to modify any aspect of his personal or economic behavior. The mountain men of the 1800's who lived in the wilderness for months at a time alone, coming in to towns only when they were forced to do so by some necessity, were extreme examples of this lonely, insistent individualism.

Each time a new territory was tamed and the less adventurous townsmen and farmers moved in, there was always a new frontier to move to. The pioneers were always beginning over again, and American social structure reflected this in its lack of permanent customs.

There was no formal movement among the frontiersman toward anarchy. But despite this, all the qualities that formed native American anarchism were there: a resistance to any authority, egoism, an assertion of individual supremacy, and an acknowledgement that men joined with their fellows voluntarily for mutual assistance.

4

The American Revolution

That only a thin line originally divided individualist anarchism from American democratic theory can best be seen by looking at the opinions held by the leaders of the early revolutionary government and by those who inspired the Revolution. Samuel Adams, Thomas Paine, Benjamin Franklin, Thomas Jefferson, even Alexander Hamilton, all had in their thinking the same elements as the early native antistatist documents. So close to anarchism did our Founding Fathers sometimes come that George Bernard Shaw was able to refer half-seriously to the United States Constitution as a conspiracy against government.

In 1729, when he was only twenty-three, Franklin published a pamphlet, *A Modest Inquiry into the Nature and Necessity of a Paper Currency*. In it he expressed a sympathy, shared by Jefferson, with the rural, agrarian elements in American life rather than with those who advocated manufacturing and commerce. The pamphlet contained one great original statement: it was the first time anyone had asserted that labor is the measure of value. In its simplest terms, this means that a thing is worth whatever it cost in labor to produce it. Here is the economic basis of American individualist antistatism that was later modified into the statement "Cost, the limit of price," by the avowed American anarchist Josiah Warren. Franklin's idea went relatively unnoticed, and it was not until forty-seven years later that the English economist Adam Smith popularized it in his *Wealth of Nations*.

The theory of voluntary association was an important one to those who advocated separation from England. Samuel Adams, taking his argument from John Locke, assumed that property was the basis of government and that men had the right to choose the way they wished to associate for its protection.

Adams was one of America's first professional agitators. After studying at Harvard with the idea of becoming a minister, young Adams chose a political career instead, and with a few friends he founded a political weekly, *The Public Advertiser*. He was especially concerned with combating the aristocracy that seemed to be arising in his native Massachusetts. There a few families with their newly acquired wealth tried to imitate the manners, dress, and morals of England. Adams feared that the next step might be the creation of an American peerage.

Before the Revolution, it was Adams' task to advocate treason daily. As a counselor to rebellion it was his responsibility to justify it and make it palatable to those who would have to support it. At one time he wrote:

Mr. Locke . . . holds that "the preservation of property is the end of government, and that for which men enter into society." It therefore necessarily supposes and requires that the people should have property. . . . Men therefore *in society having property,* they have the right to the goods, which by the law of the community are theirs, that nobody hath the right to take *any part* of their subsistence from them without their consent: without this, they could have no property at all, for I truly can have no property in that which another can by right take from me when he pleases, against my consent. Hence, says he, it is a mistake to think that the supreme power of any commonwealth can dispose of the estate of the subject arbitrarily, or *take any part* of them at pleasure. The prince or senate can never have a power to take to themselves the whole or any part of the subjects' property without *their own* consent; for this would be in effect to have no property at all.[1]

The next question then might be: why should a man consent to government at all if he can protect his property by other means?

As one American anarchist, Voltarine de Cleyre (1866–1913), pointed out, the goal of those who made the Revolution was to change political institutions in order to make the government not a separate, controlling, fearful thing but a serviceable agent "responsible, economical, and trustworthy . . . for the transaction of such business as was the common concern, and to set the limits of the common concern at the line where no man's liberty would enroach upon another's."[2]

In other words, equal liberty is a practical goal for a modern society, the same sociological stand as that of the anarchists. The difference lies in the democrat's belief that the best way to obtain equal liberty is in the rule and decision of the majority.

Several other basic elements of democracy are shared by the projected anarchist community of the antistatists: the reliance on local government or federation rather than on one central governing body; a ridding of local government from tyrannical institutions; and the conviction that free federations are possible only when there are free communities to federate.

Although Adams was an effective spokesman, the greatest propagandist for the American Revolution was Thomas Paine (1738–1809), who gave his allegiance to no nation. "The world is my country. . . . To do good is my religion," he wrote, and throughout his life, Paine tried to put his ideals into practice.

THOMAS PAINE

The New York Public Library

Born in Norfolk, England, of a Quaker family, Paine went to sea for a few years as a young man and then settled in London. He insisted on expressing his opinions by any means possible. Among his uncomfortable views were opposition to Negro slavery, advocacy of divorce, and a stand in favor of women's rights. Paine rapidly lost his reputation and found enemies accumulating with equal speed. Tories in their clubs showed TP nails in their boot heels as demonstrations that they trampled on his principles.

Unhappily married and unsuccessful in business, Tom Paine separated from his wife and lost all his goods to creditors. At Benjamin Franklin's urging, he decided to settle in America, arriving in 1774 at the age of thirty-seven.

From the beginning, Paine was wholeheartedly with the rebels. Only thirteen months after his arrival in Philadelphia, Paine published *Common Sense,* which roused men to action against the English. Paine's unavowed though apparent antistatism was clear in *Common Sense.* In one passage he said:

> Some writers have so confounded society with government as to leave little or no distinction between them; whereas they are not only different, but have different origins. Society is produced by our wants, and government by our wickedness; the former promotes our happiness *positively* by uniting our affections, the latter *negatively* by restraining our vices. . . .
>
> Society is in every state a blessing, but government, even in its best state is but a necessary evil; in its worst state an intolerable one; for when we suffer or are exposed to the same miseries by a *government* which we might expect in a country without government, our calamity is heightened by reflecting that we furnish the means by which we suffer. Government, like dress, is the badge of lost innocence; the palaces of kings are built on the ruins of the bowers of paradise.[3]

Paine went on to note that it is common interest that holds men together, and the laws ordained by common usage have a greater weight than those established by governments, which hinder the natural development of society.

After the Revolution, Paine did not abandon his reflections on government and society. He went back to England, where he became acquainted with William Godwin and was a strong influence on that anarchist's ideas. Along with Jefferson he found it impossible to take a positive stand about government, law, and its enforcement; these were simply necessary, albeit arbitrary, needs of society. The State was useful only because it was expedient. If government was of a type that was good for the citizens, then and only then could it be justified. But as men progressed, learning that they had to cooperate for their own self-interest, they would be able to do so without any formal regulation. "Society is capable of performing for itself almost all the functions which are ordinarily assigned to the government, and is constantly teaching us to reduce further the number of government functions."[4]

As an example, Paine cited the American Revolution where, "in the absence of any regular government, the identity of interests was sufficient to bring about common security."[5] The abolition of all kinds of authoritarianism, no matter how benevolent, would not result in the dissolution of society but rather in the strengthening of the social bond. It is governments, founded by robbers, usurpers, and conquerors, that are antisocial, making war in order to justify their existence.

While the propagandists of the Revolution were important to its success, equally vital was a surety on the part of the Americans that the rebellion had not been fomented for selfish reasons. If any man speaks to the world of the intellectual power and moral rectitude of the architects of the Revolution and the Constitution, it is Thomas Jefferson. Significantly, he was born not in a long-settled urban section of the colonies but in the frontier region of Virginia, on the edge of the Blue Ridge Mountains, the son of a pioneer.

Jefferson was convinced that the only possible basis for a true democracy was an agricultural society. Mercantilism he regarded only as a threat and a possible destroyer of the democratic state. Jefferson was an exponent of the frontiersman's desire for economy and simplicity in government, the right of the individual to his own beliefs—even if such beliefs entail rebellion—and the essential freedom of the individual. To him, the ideal America was a land of "free upstanding farmers with just enough government to keep order among them."[6]

In a letter to Madison, Jefferson wrote:

Societies exist under three forms sufficiently distinguishable. 1. Without government as among an Indian's; 2. Under government wherein the will of everyone has a just influence; as is the case in England to a slight degree, and in our States in a great one; 3. Under government of force as in the case of all other monarchies, and in most of the other republics. To have an idea of the curse of existence in these last, they must be seen. It is a government of sheep over wolves. It is a problem not clear in my mind that the first condition is not the best. But I believe it to be inconsistent with any great degree of population.[7]

The supposed anarchical state of the Indian interested Jefferson more than once and helped to contribute to his doubt as to the efficacy of government. In another letter, this one to Edward Carrington, in 1787, he wrote:

The basis of our government being the opinion of the people, the very first object should be to keep that right; and were it left to me to decide whether we should have a government without newspapers, or newspapers without government, I should not hesitate a moment to prefer the latter, but I should mean that every man should receive those papers and be capable of reading them. I am convinced that those societies (as the Indians) which live without government, enjoy in their general mass an infinitely greater degree of happiness than those who live under the European governments. Among the former, public opinion is in the place of law, and restrains morals as inexorably as laws ever did anywhere. Among the latter, under the pretence of governing, they have divided their nations into two classes, wolves and sheep.[8]

Jefferson's doubts about government were created because he was confronting the problem of many who begin by questioning the right of arbitrary authoritarian government and end by suspecting that the only justification for any rule at all is the sheer necessity to keep order among a large population. As he put it, "It is error alone which needs the support of government. Truth can stand by itself."[9] Not without justice, the noted American historian Charles Beard called Jefferson's viewpoint "his doctrine of anarchy plus the police constable."[10]

While at work on the Declaration of Independence and the

Constitution, Jefferson bore before him at all times his certainty that "that government is best which governs least." The State must never, he felt, be allowed to interfere in the personal affairs of its citizens—to which idea we may be grateful for our Bill of Rights and the careful constitutional protection of the freedom, insomuch as possible, of each citizen of the United States.

On education, too, Jefferson and the anarchists share the same position. In 1782 he wrote, "In every government on earth there is some trace of human weakness, some germ of corruption and degeneracy, . . . Every government degenerates when trusted to the rulers of the people alone. The people themselves, therefore, are its only safe depositories. And to render even them safe, their minds must be improved to a certain degree. . . ."[11]

Traditionally, native individualist anarchists and the American conservatives have drawn their arguments from much the same sentiment and rationale. And in regard to the justification of government, some of the more conservative of the early American political figures were in agreement with Jefferson and Paine. During the great debate over the Constitution and what it should contain, it seemed for a time that agreement on any federal structure might never be reached. To propagandize in favor of the document that was being submitted to soon-to-be-states, Alexander Hamilton, certainly one of the least libertarian of the new republicans, and James Madison wrote a series of papers, *The Federalist,* which became a basic element in American political theory.

Both Hamilton and Madison justified the existence of the State in the same way. Such sanction was not to be found in good will, in any divinely ordained structure of society, nor in self-interest. It could be found only in *coercion,* which is necessary because of the universal sinfulness and selfishness of man. Even in *The Federalist,* the ultimate defense of the Constitution, no greater argument could be found. Thus, Number 15 asked, "Why has government been instituted at all? Because the passions of men will not conform to the dictates of reason and justice, without restraint."

Once the necessary coercive powers have been given to the

State, it must supply its own methods of giving equal rights to its citizens and justice to all.

It is at this point that the American anarchist, like all his philosophical comrades, fails. Fine though his dissection of the evils of the State and government may be, unanswerable though his ethical stand may be, he does not recognize the practical necessities of day-to-day living: in particular his ideal no-government community almost always fails to take into account the problems presented by massive population and modern technological advance. If the United States had stayed as it was in the time of Jefferson, about ninety per cent agrarian, or even equally divided between a rural and urban population, some sort of evolutionary progress toward a voluntary, governmentless society might have been made. That may be why, aside from a few feeble attempts at the formation of Utopian communities, American individualist anarchism has remained an intellectual force rather than a movement committed to action as its European counterpart was and is.

5

The Rise of Individualist Anarchism

The Revolution over and the Constitution successfully adopted, the United States settled into preparing the way for economic and industrial progress. With the election of Jefferson to the presidency in 1800, the liberals seemed destined to be at the helm of American political life. The frontier was being pushed forward every year, and on its edge, or immediately in its wake, thrived the farmer and small merchant enjoying the "right to life, liberty, and the pursuit of happiness" that had been so hard won.

The westward-moving throngs may not at first have been aware of the new impetus being given to American life. Factory production was increasing in any way possible. The cry of the industrialists was for laissez-faire capitalism, for business left alone, unimpeded by any restrictions. In the cities the last vestiges of rural life were disappearing, but on the frontier, for several generations the new social forces of the East might just as easily not have existed. Only slowly did it come to the pioneers that their America, the land of the unfettered self-made man free from the domination of wealth or class, the land of endless opportunities, was disappearing.

Filled with confidence in the potentiality of their newly created land, a wave of romanticism possessed the middle class, the pioneers, and the capitalist barons of industry. The romantic view of the world was inevitably optimistic and involved a confidence in the eventual attainment of perfection on earth. It was a direct source of individualist anarchism.

The link between antistatism and romanticism is a close one. Voltarine de Cleyre pointed out that one major reason for her involvement in the anarchist movement was the fact that she possessed a large proportion of sentiment. This, a fascination with nature, and an interest in the moral perfection of man are typical of both modes of thought.

Even the romantic belief in the nearness and potentiality of a new social order is inherent in early American history. The great seal of America, adopted after the Revolution, contains the motto, *Novis Ordo Seclorum*, "A new order of the ages." And for many living in the United States today, this concept of their country as a savior of the world, and as a bringer of new tidings, is still viable. Edward Johnson, one of the colonists in Massachusetts wrote that New England would be "a specimen of what shall be over all the earth in the glorious times that are expected."[1] The native anarchist had only to add to the argument that the great new society had not yet been born.

That these characteristics were all dominant in American life is attested to by a particularly acute observer of the life in the new country. On May 11, 1831, Alexis Charles Henri Clérel de Tocqueville (1805–1859)—a French descendant of a minor noble family, in his twenties, curious, fair-minded, and extremely observant—landed at Manhattan from the steamer *President*. His ostensible mission, given him by the French government, was to study the prison system in the United States. But de Tocqueville had already decided that his central aim on this visit would be to write honestly on the new democracy. His trenchant epitome of the American character in *Democracy in America* has never been superseded.

What did de Tocqueville see? Complete independence: "Of all the political effects produced by this equality of condition, this love of independence is the first to strike the observing and to alarm the timid; nor can it be said that their alarm is wholly misplaced, for anarchy has a more formidable aspect in democratic countries than elsewhere."[2]

Self-interest: "Americans . . . show with complacency how an enlightened regard for themselves constantly prompts them to assist one another and inclines them willingly to sacrifice a portion of their time and property to the welfare of the state."[3]

Individualism as a result of self-interest and equality: "Our fathers were only acquainted with égoïsme [selfishness]. Selfishness is a passionate and exaggerated love of self, which leads a man to connect everything with himself and to prefer himself to everything in the world. Individualism is a mature and calm feeling, which disposes each member of the community to sever himself from the mass of his fellows and to draw apart with his family and friends, so that after he has thus formed a little circle of his own he willingly leaves society at large to itself."[4]

Along with the individualism and classlessness of the new society went an odd kind of loneliness: "Not only does democracy make every man forget his ancestors, but it hides his descendants and separates his contemporaries from him; it throws him back forever upon himself alone and threatens in the end to confine him entirely within the solitude of his own heart."[5]

He also realized the importance of townships and local rule in opposition to governmental centralism in American political structure. Thus, "the township was organized before the county, the county before the state, the state before the union."[6] And, later: "The village or township is the only association which is so perfectly natural that, wherever a number of men are collected, it seems to constitute itself."[7]

Finally, de Tocqueville, who might have seemed to pave the way for a justification of individualist anarchism, points out why it will never exist in the United States. It is universally acknowledged in this country that the sovereignty of the individual is primary; he must have the power to be his own arbiter and the sole judge of his private interest. Further, society has no right, in America, to interfere in any man's actions unless they may harm the common good.

Despite this, de Tocqueville goes on, men do still yield to the State and willingly allow its laws to govern them. It is the free institutions of the country, along with the emphasis on local rule and responsibility, that combats the urge toward anarchy. "I am convinced that anarchy is not the principal evil that democratic ages have to fear, but the least. For the principle of equality begets two tendencies: the one leads men straight to independence and may suddenly drive them into anarchy; the other conducts them by a longer, more secret, but more certain road to servitude. Nations readily discern the former tendency and are prepared to resist it; they are led away by the latter, without perceiving its drift; hence it is peculiarly important to point it out."[8]

Before going on to a discussion of the first avowed individualist anarchist, Josiah Warren, it will be helpful to explore the writings of Emerson and Thoreau, two early antistatists, and then look at the general doctrines of native antistatism.

A father of American literature, Ralph Waldo Emerson (1803 –1882) was also the most searching critic of his time. Emerson was aware that he had a mission to analyze and evaluate the civilization he saw around him. From his youth, he was gentle, introspective, and a thoughtful student, with one goal in life: to invest his time wisely. Even his early journals are a diary of an already complex mental life. And his cheerfulness and serenity of character gave him the patience to devote endless amounts of energy to the study and practice necessary to develop his prose style and the logicality of the thoughts expressed in it.

RALPH WALDO EMERSON

The New York Public Library

Emerson justified the sovereignty of the individual by appeals to religion. As the commentator on American thought, Vernon Parrington, wrote: "The universe he conceived of as a divine whole, whereof each man is his own center from whom flows the life that has flowed in upon him. . . . The law for things is not the law for mind; man is unkinged in acknowledging any lesser sovereignty than the sovereignty of self. Statutes, constitutions, governments, schools, churches, banks, trade—the coercing sum of institutions and customs—these things do not signify; they are only idols with clay feet that bind men to worship. The true divinity dwells elsewhere, in the soul of man; and that divinity must rule the world and not be ruled by it."[9]

Emerson found society mean and ignoble, and the ends it pursued equally reprehensible. The cause for this was not individual man, but social institutions themselves, which served only to encourage the baser instincts of men. The State and its laws always were enemies of liberty and morality. "Every actual State is corrupt. Good men must not obey the laws too well. . . . Wild liberty develops iron conscience. Want of liberty, by strengthening law and decorum, stupefies conscience."[10]

So, concerned with what the ideal of a republic should be, he formed a speculative theory of politics which borders on philosophical anarchism. Constitutions, laws, checks and balances, Emerson discards, finding that the only true basis on which a republic is founded is good will. Once sensible men recognize that voluntary cooperation to protect their common interest is necessary, good government is possible, but not until then. This lack of recognition is the cause of man's tragic failure to achieve a sane political state.

By a simple extension, morality is derived from the individual's own good will and sense of identity. He can recognize others' right and wrong by his own sense of them. And when he tries to exert domination over others, he has overstepped the truth and entered into a false relationship.

This is the history of governments,—one man does something which is to bind another. A man who cannot be acquainted with me, taxes me; looking from afar at me ordains that a part of my labor shall go to this or that whimsical end,—not as I, but as he happens to fancy. . . . Hence the less government we have the better,—the fewer laws and the less confined power. The antidote to this abuse of formal government is the influence of private character, the growth of the individual . . . the appearance of the wise man; of whom the existing government is, it must be owned, but a shabby imitation. The tendencies of the times favor the idea of self-government, and leave the individual to the rewards and penalties of his own constitution.[11]

Like Jefferson, Emerson was unhappy with the new industrialism. Nor was he sure that the division of labor upon which it was based was a good or necessarily final system. He went so far as to suggest that each man have his own farm or craft, pursued independently of anyone else's work. Emerson was appalled at the materialism of the new American mercantile spirit, and slavery was morally offensive to him. The more he investigated his contemporary society, the less he could accept it. In 1837, he wrote in his journal: "The present generation is bankrupt of principles and hope as of property. . . . He is a tassel at the apron-string of society. . . . As far back as I can see the widening procession of humanity, the marchers are lame and blind and deaf."[12]

Confronted with intolerable conditions, exasperated and depressed by a society that seems to be moving farther and farther from what is right and decent, a man may sit at home writing intelligently in his journal or he can decide to act in support of his philosophy. Emerson chose the former. It remained for his good friend and literary colleague, Henry David Thoreau (1817–1862), to make the first anarchist demonstration against government in the United States. Weak and transitory though it was, Thoreau's gesture of defiance was historic. His protest and the subsequent *On the Duty of Civil Disobedience* succeeded in focusing and making apparent the latent element of anarchism in American political thought almost from the time of the first settlers.

HENRY DAVID THOREAU

The New York Public Library

Up until Thoreau's time, men would have agreed that government was unsatisfactory, immoral, and oppressive, but most
would also have accepted as an obvious conclusion the fact that
some government—albeit as little as possible—was necessary and
that a citizen owed his country the duty of civil obedience.
Thoreau took the final step. If the best government is the least
government, then absolutely the best government is that which
doesn't exist at all.

Thoreau, irascible, known generally as an odd, eccentric individual, had a passionate love of nature which eventually led
him to spend the years 1845–1847 in retreat at Walden, Mas-
sachussetts, where he built his own house and provided his own
food. Born and bred in nearby Concord, he seemed to be nour-
ished by his native soil in surroundings that fed his curious mind.
Although he lived within only a few miles of Boston, Thoreau—
almost to the point of neuroticism—distrusted the city and its

environment, like a true anarchist finding his solace only in the countryside.

With an astonishing egoism, Thoreau set about finding how to live the good life, how he could obtain the optimal freedom of self and soul. Once he determined what the moral procedure in any one situation would be, he would follow it. "To be a philosopher is not merely to have subtle thoughts, . . . but so to love wisdom as to live according to its dictates, a life of simplicity, independence, magnanimity, and trust. It is to solve some of the problems of life, not only theoretically, but practically."[13]

An increasing obstacle to individual freedom was to be found in the economic bondage imposed on almost every member of society by the new technology. In his search for a way to universal economic freedom Thoreau developed a strong antagonism to all kinds of authoritarianism.

At Walden, he at first removed himself from active participation in society in an attempt to work out his own salvation by himself. But he frequently went into Concord village, and there he was horrified in 1846 to find his neighbors drilling and preparing for the war with Mexico, which lasted from May of that year until 1848. Basic objections to war as such were reinforced because to Thoreau, as to many of the liberals of his time, this battle was the more hateful, stupid, and unjust because it had as one of its inevitable ends the extension of Negro slavery, to which Thoreau was unalterably opposed.

Up to this point Thoreau had reconciled himself to leaving the government alone if it would do the same for him. But when a constable came to him and demanded that he pay a tax that would go toward paying the costs of the Mexican War, which was morally impossible for him to support, Thoreau had to confront his conscience. He could not compromise, nor could he ethically pay the tax and then retreat to Walden, cursing society from there. The only sensible solution seemed to be a kind of passive resistance; so he first refused to pay this tax, as he had refused to pay a church tax some years earlier, and then retired to Walden to meditate on the subject.

This anarchistic refusal to recognize the superior sovereignty of his government could not go unpunished, and Thoreau allowed himself to be removed peaceably to the Concord town jail. Even jail was not too much to bear in order to live as strictly as possible by one's philosophy. A probably apocryphal tale has it that during his short stay in prison, Thoreau was visited by Emerson, who, horrified that his good friend should be in such straits cried, "Henry, what are you doing in there." The answer by Thoreau: "Waldo, what are *you* doing out there?"[14]

The punishment was brief—only one night in jail. The next day his friends intervened, as they had in the earlier case, and paid the tax in question. And though he continued to refuse further tax payments, Thoreau was never jailed again for this or any other act of civil disobedience. The time in prison could not have been more brief, yet it was enough. When he came out he said, "I saw that the state was half-witted, and it was as timid as a lone woman with her silver spoons, and that it did not know its friends from its foes, and I lost all my remaining respect for it and pitied it."[15]

Thoreau had become a philosophic anarchist. On his return to Walden, he continued to be concerned with the implication of his refusal to pay the taxes and his subsequent jailing. The result was *On the Duty of Civil Disobedience,* an uncompromising assertion of the primary sovereignty of the individual. Because of expedience, he, too, had to accept that the government could not immediately be eliminated, but he wrote:

That government is best which governs not at all; and when men are prepared for it, that will be the kind of government which they will have. Government is at best but an expedient; but most governments are usually, and all governments are sometimes, inexpedient.

A government in which the majority rule in all cases cannot be based on justice. . . . How does a man behave toward this American government today? I answer that he cannot without disgrace be associated with it. . . . It is not a man's duty as a matter of course, to devote himself to the eradication of any, even the most enormous wrong; he may still properly have other concerns to engage him; but it is his duty, at least, to wash his hands of it, . . . If the law is of such a nature that it requires you to be an agent of injustice to another, then, I say, break the law. Let your life be a counter friction to stop the machine.[16]

Thoreau made a personal statement as well, saying that he wished to refuse his allegiance to the State, "to withdraw and stand aloof from it . . . In fact, I quietly declare war with the State, after my fashion, though I will still make what use and get what advantage of her I can, as is usual in such cases."[17] In short, "My thoughts are murder to the state."

Most of the early native anarchists in the United States had, like Emerson and Thoreau, inherited the colonial American independence. As one of their number, Ezra Heywood, claimed, "Anarchism is only a new assertion of the ideas of self-rule and self-support which Jefferson put into the Declaration of Independence in 1776, and Josiah Warren's doctrine of the sovereignty of the individual on the basis of the cost principle only sets forth a natural proposal of this fundamental."[18]

When successful attempts were made to restrict immigration into the United States during the last years of the nineteenth century and first quarter of the twentieth, one of the major arguments of those in favor of such laws was that radicals such as anarchists and communists were entering the country and corrupting its citizens with their foreign ideas. Certainly, as will be seen later, the anarchist immigrants were responsible for the three most notorious episodes in antistatism in this country: the Haymarket riot, the Sacco-Vanzetti case, and the assassination of President McKinley.

This was a comforting fact to those who regarded anarchism as a purely alien phenomenon. Yet, as one writer has pointed out: "Anarchism is a product of democracy. It is as much at home on American soil as on European. The general belief to the contrary is one of the survivals of the notion that Providence has vouchsafed us a peculiar care and an especial enlightenment. If we wished to argue that anarchism is a peculiar and characteristic American product, reasons would not be lacking."[19]

Not only was American romanticism an ideal field for antistatist thought to flourish in, but the economic and social changes of the early 1800's encouraged the trend. The rising factories discouraged, and in fact penalized, independent action. Instead of determining the worth of their own products, men had to sell their labor for a price set by someone else. Men who as boys had grown up in the country lanes on the outskirts of cities, now saw sidewalks, tall buildings, and factories gradually encroaching on their land. Families were being crowded into the spiritually eroding slums. So the antistatists cried out for a return to the peace and tranquillities of the past. As Dorothy Day wrote: "They were lambs in the simplicity of their program. They wanted to see the grass spring up between the cobbles of the city streets. They wanted to see the workers leave the cities with their wives and children and take to the fields, build themselves homes, where they would have room to breathe, to study, to pray, where there could be work for all."[20]

One peculiarly American hope was held out to the rising numbers of the proletariat. There were always unsettled lands to the west that could be reached if only a man saved enough money to take his family there. Indeed, the student of American Utopian communities, Charles Nordhoff, writing in 1875, thought that this was the guiding motivation behind the government's urge to acquire more territory. For if only one worker in a thousand took advantage of the public lands, his comrades all knew that they might do so, and this made them more content with their increasingly unhappy lot. "Any circumstance," said Nordhoff, "[such] as the exhaustion of these lands, which should materially impair this opportunity for independence would be, I believe, a serious calamity to our country."[21]

As pointed out earlier, once the new settlers took advantage of the free land, they were alone. It is a fact that they got only as much law as they wanted or needed. Even when a sheriff or marshal managed to create some sort of authority structure, he still had to depend on the town's public opinion and good will when he needed a posse. One commentator wrote: "On the Western frontier, the general will, like the political equality of all [white] men, was no fiction of a political philosopher, but an observable reality."[22]

The pioneer had to face another unique situation, one important in the formation of individualist anarchism. Since the settlers were isolated from all the apparatus of the East, they had to make new economic arrangements. Money was not always the most satisfactory means of settling bargains or arriving at contractual terms, and a spirit of mutualism and barter replaced the more artificial economic structures of the cities. Men gave and received personal credit of all sorts—for courage, for some sort of ability, for hard work, for potential economic or service returns.

Individualist anarchism is primarily an intellectual movement. In fact, the founders of this native antistatism called it "scientific anarchism." They had studied the progress the physical sciences had suddenly made. It seemed as though within time all the laws of the universe would be discovered. All the phenomena of life would be explained in inviolable and nonmoral terms. To the individualists, the function of the political philosopher was to incorporate these laws, as they were discovered, into society. The laws of nature were certain facts and as such supplanted the laws of God. (In their insistence on natural law and its importance, the anarchists once more shared the sentiments of conservative thinkers.)

While the individualist anarchists might disagree with one another on minor points, they agreed on a number of major ones:

Any kind of collective society leads to authoritarianism, expressed by government and laws, which is destructive and inimical to the fulfillment of the human personality.

Private property, so long as it is only the total worth of an individual's labor, is one of his rights.

Individual freedom, the sovereignty of the individual, and its preservation is the purpose of society. When the State curbs this sovereignty, it is wrong, and since the State exists only by nature of such curbs it should be eliminated.

Since the individual should always have complete freedom, any inequality between the sexes is artificial and wrong. Women should have equal rights in politics, economics, and sexual behavior, with no exception. The same equality should be extended to other races, and insofar as they existed, among all classes.

Each man should receive only the product of his own labor. Rent, interest, dividends, capital profits—all were violations of this principle and should be eliminated.

Free competition (the laissez-faire philosophy of the conservative capitalist) is an expression of individual sovereignty and should not be impeded as long as men did not try to get more than their labor was worth.

When men joined together, ideally they did so voluntarily in order to benefit each other mutually and to protect the result of their labor. This association, since it would be voluntary, could be discarded by any individual as he so desired. Moreover, the selfish interest of each individual protected him from succumbing to oppression by any other individual.

Democracy is based on the rule of the majority. Yet by doing so it intrudes on the natural rights of the sovereignty of the minority party or individual. When even one individual does not consent to a policy or action and it is implemented despite his objection, he is oppressed. Therefore democracy as such must be destroyed as just another form of authoritarian government.

Finally, since no authority should exist without the consent of the individual, civil disobedience, nonviolent resistance, and, in certain rare cases, destruction of property were considered by the individualist anarchist to be legitimate weapons in the battle against the State. But he never accepted the "propaganda by deed" of the immigrant antistatist, regarding it as gratuitous and immoral.

6

Josiah Warren

One of the odd manifestations of the romantic spirit in American life was the appearance throughout the nineteenth century of more than one hundred Utopian communities. The urge to establish a perfect society that is philosophically compatible with some moral system is ancient, going back at least as far as Plato. When a man, after great and painful contemplation, becomes aware that the world as it exists is full of evil, when, moreover, he develops an ideal of his own that he is sure will revolutionize the state of mankind and usher in a new social order, it is hard for him not to want to implement that ideal, no matter on how small a scale.

The somewhat cranky individualism of the United States in the 1800's encouraged men to believe that they might be messiahs, granting through their efforts a glimpse of the millennium to the faithful. The Puritans and other early settlers had come to the colonies, after all, out of a Utopian urge.

The structure of the communities varied greatly. Some, such as that of the Rappites at Harmony, Indiana, were religious in nature; others—for example, the famous Brook Farm, were socialistic; a few were anarchistic. The economy of the Utopian efforts ran the gamut from private ownership to totally communal living, and sexual life among them fluctuated from celibacy to free love and polygamy. Some of the leaders were charlatans, some were fanatics, some were sincere idealists. Only one group, the Church of the Latter Day Saints, or Mormons, made a lasting and important impression on American life that exists to this day. And even the Mormons eventually had to compromise their ideals in order to coexist with an American society in which polygamy is considered sinful and illegal.

For those believers in antistatism, the call to action was great. Since the individualists advocated a withdrawal from the State, what better way was there to effect this condition than to establish instead of the State a Utopian community where men could voluntarily create a nonauthoritarian society. Josiah Warren's collision with a Utopia—in this case socialistic in nature—at New Harmony, Indiana, was probably the most important single event in his life.

Josiah Warren (1798–1874) was born in Boston, two years after the first great anarchist treatise, William Godwin's *Political Justice*, was first published in Philadelphia. The Warren family was of old Puritan stock, and Josiah grew up surrounded by the New England Yankee traditions. He was an optimistic boy, noted for his wit and ingenuity as well as a remarkable musical talent. While still youths, Josiah and his brother had been members of the "Old Boston Brigade Band."

The twenty-year-old Josiah Warren, thickset, intense, with strong, restless blue eyes, must have been a memorable suitor. In 1818 he married Caroline Cutter, and the next year the young Warrens moved to Cincinnati where Josiah had a job as an orchestra leader, as well as playing and teaching music.

Warren was ambitious and inventive. He developed an outstanding new type of lamp that burned lard instead of oil or tallow, resulting in cheaper and better illumination; to manufacture his invention the young musician set up a factory that immediately prospered. Over the years Josiah also contributed to the advancement of the printing press and to musical notation.

During this early work, Warren had probably been reading liberal and radical literature. For whatever reason, he was ready for the most decisive encounter of his life when it occurred, in 1825. Robert Owen, a Welsh millionaire and philanthropist, who was something of an eccentric, had come to the Midwest to found a Utopian community based on his socialistic philosophy. Owen had purchased Harmony, the site of the Rappist community in Indiana, and had renamed it New Harmony. Whatever Owen said to the young Warren, their first meeting turned the musician to the career of radicalism.

In the fall of 1825, Warren began to take an active part in the planning of the colony and worked on drafting the first constitution, adopted by the community in February of 1826. By that time, Warren was completely committed to Owen's ideas. He sold the lamp factory and moved his family to New Harmony in February or March of 1826.

The family lived at New Harmony for more than a year. During this time, Josiah's duties in the colony included conducting a weekly concert of the New Harmony band. His work left him plenty of time to observe the decline and growing dissension in the group, typical of Utopian experiments.

Warren was greatly affected by the failure of this community. His faith in the possibilities of developing an ideal social group, however, was not shaken. Rather, he felt that the economic basis of New Harmony—socialism—was at fault. He was convinced that property held in common by the entire community could not work. Instead, the goal should be the voluntary association of individuals, each with private property equal to the value of

New Harmony at the time of Warren's residence there

Culver Pict

his own labor. To each man should be opened freely, under equal conditions, all the natural wealth of the country—land, minerals, water, and so on.

At New Harmony, he thought, the individual had been submerged in the community, sacrificing his sovereignty to an alien authority. Once this submersion began, Warren believed, a lack of initiative set in and was encouraged by each person's lack of responsibility and subsequent failure to desire progress. Men had to have a chance to be the free, diverse creatures nature had intended them to be. Of the experience, he wrote: "It seemed that the differences of opinion, taste, and purposes *increased* just in proportion to the demand for conformity. . . . It was nature's own inherent law of DIVERSITY that had conquered us. . . . Our own 'united interests' were directly at war with the INDIVIDU-ALITIES of persons and circumstances and the instinct of self-preservation."[1]

The economic basis of individual sovereignty was that the true price of anything was the amount of labor spent on providing it; this Warren decided early in his libertarian career. After the New Harmony debacle he decided to put the idea into effect. In 1827, returning to Cincinnati, he opened on May 18 a Time Store, which continued to function until 1830. This was the first commercial cooperative market ever to be established and modern co-ops are loosely based on its pattern. Josiah believed that if the Time Store were successful, it could serve as the means for a slow, peaceful transition from capitalism to a governmentless, "labor for labor" economy.

The store's original stock was $300 worth of groceries and dry goods. In order to make it perfectly clear to his customers that all the merchandise was priced in accord with the same rigid rules, Josiah posted the bills of purchase for all the goods. A buyer could consult them before checking the store price, which would always be the original cost of the article plus 7 per cent (later lowered to 4 per cent) for "contingent expenses." This small additional charge was never intended to supply any profit for the proprietor. Instead it was a surcharge to cover shipping expenses and store overhead.

That Warren labored by establishing the store, ordering the goods, unpacking them on their arrival, keeping inventory, and selling them, was, however, an inescapable fact. Just as no man should be paid without having labored, so no man's labor should go unpaid. Josiah Warren's labor was no exception. In order to receive due compensation, Warren developed—borrowing somewhat from Owen—the idea of the "labor note." This was to be paper money, independently issued, for the use of the voluntary participants in the Time Store plan. Instead of being an equivalent of gold or sterling reserves, as our national currency now is, the basic unit of the labor note was a given weight of corn or its equivalent in labor. A carpenter could pay off his labor notes in time spent building shelves in the store, for example; a shoemaker could make Mrs. Warren a pair of shoes, or, if that would take more time than his labor notes demanded, resole an old pair.

This was a startling departure in merchandising. For the first time, the proprietor's payment was separated from the price of the goods and was independent of their intrinsic worth. In Warren's reasoning, it was not possible to assign an arbitrary percentage to be added to the cost of all goods to repay him for his labor in operating the Time Store. A markup of 20 per cent on needles would be remarkably small; yet if woolens were marked up by that amount there would be a profit beyond the income to which Warren's labor entitled him.

Apparently the only logical standard of payment was the amount of time it took to sell something. This made practical sense. Quite literally, time was money. If a hundred barrels of flour took the same time to sell as two yards of cloth or five needles, the payment for all the sales would be the same, and it would be based on the only true and fair scale, the amount of time the purchase took. Warren put a clock up in the store so that it could always be checked by the customers. He also had a clock dial, on which the hands were set at the time the sale started. When the business was completed and the merchandise changed hands, the elapsed time was recorded. This time was then multiplied by two (to give some fair consideration to Warren's purchase and stocking of the goods) and equivalent labor notes changed hands. Naturally, the customers took as little of Warren's time as possible and stopped haggling over prices. This freed him to handle more purchases in shorter periods.

While at first sight the concept of the labor note seems peculiar and eccentric, it had sound economic sense behind it. Also, at this time, there was no standard national money. Commercial banks all over the country were issuing their own scrip. A national currency, rigidly regulated throughout the country, was not successfully effected until 1866.

The Time Store was not immediately popular. Warren's innovations were regarded with a certain suspicion. So in order to supplement his income, the musician gave lessons at night. The payment for these was in labor notes. But the Cincinnatians soon began to see that they were getting more for their money at Mr. Warren's Time Store, and patronage steadily increased. By the end of the first year the capacity of the store was doubled. Other services were added. Customers began to post notices in the store of material or services they needed. Craftsmen who could furnish the necessary labor checked the lists and then arranged to be paid in goods they in turn wanted.

One would expect the still-young Warren to take pleasure in his success, perhaps to contemplate the opening of a chain of Time Stores, and to settle down tranquilly with his family. But Josiah Warren was still not a contented man. At first, what bothered him was a general inequity in the way labor was paid for. Sensibly, laborers doing the most unpleasant kinds of work—cleaning the streets, for example—should be paid more for their chores than those who did more palatable tasks—being cashier in a bank, perhaps. But in the business world, the reverse was true, and men benefited by choosing the less onerous jobs. In order to compensate for this, Warren tried to give more labor notes per hour for the less pleasant tasks done for him.

Even so, he was restless. His pioneer spirit was in need of a further frontier. All around him the America into which he had been born was changing; a spirit of social reform was in the air. The United States was still in flux, and a new social order might yet be established. The Time Store had clearly been shown to be a successful project; those who wanted to have one in their communities knew how it would operate. So it had no more interest for Warren, and he closed it in May of 1830.

Beyond everything, the consuming idea in Warren's mind was the building of a society without authority where the freedom of the individual was the major factor. The implementation of "labor for labor" was only one aspect of this. He later wrote: "Society must be so converted as to preserve the SOVEREIGNTY OF EVERY INDIVIDUAL inviolate. That is it must avoid all combinations and connections of persons and interests and all other arrangements which will not leave every individual at all times at liberty to dispose of his or her person, and time, and property in any manner in which his or her feelings of judgment may dictate, WITHOUT INVOLVING THE PERSON OR INTERESTS OF OTHERS."[2]

The next step seemed clear, and in fact Warren had already begun planning for it in the year before the store was closed. If he could so easily demonstrate the value of the labor-for-labor principle by setting up and running a store, why not set up and run a community based on his larger ideas—social as well as economic? Granted his experience at New Harmony had been unfortunate, it had only taught him the better ways to establish an anarchist settlement.

Ohio seemed to be the best choice for a community, but Robert Owen's son persuaded Josiah that New York would be a more fruitful environment. Unfortunately, by the time the store closed, the investors lost interest and the New York plans fell through. For the next several years Warren spent his time refining his anarchist philosophy and working with machinery again. His improvements in the printing press led to a much cheaper process of multiple copies than had been hitherto possible.

Warren still used every opportunity to put his theories to pragmatic tests. Even his family was not immune from "labor for labor." Josiah's son told a friend that his father never let him have his breakfast before he had earned it. The Warren children, equal in his eyes to anyone else, were paid on the same basis as adults for their work.

Typically, once he had developed the improved printing technique, Warren set about using it. In 1833 he started in Cincinnati a four-page weekly, *The Peaceful Revolutionist*, which he wrote, set into type, and printed on his own press. It was the first anarchist newspaper to appear anywhere in the world.

Nothing seemed to satisfy his restless intellect. He began at this time to study the semantics theories of Alexander Bryan Johnson. What he learned gave him new arguments for his feelings about the oppressiveness of the State. Warren began to argue that government and law were not material objects, but rather forms of language. Since this was so, like any word structures, they could be defined in different ways by different persons, and then interpreted and put into effect accordingly.

Warren had just started the weekly when he got yet another idea. His thoughts went back to earlier plans for the establishment of a Utopian anarchist community, and he immediately began implementing the project. Under his leadership a small group was formed and a site of four hundred acres along the Tuscarora River in Ohio was purchased. There, in 1835, six families set up the Village of Equity. Again, Warren was the first to see that anarchism, like a scientific hypothesis, had to be tested practically; this community was probably the first antistatist Utopia in the Western world.

Practical problems were solved quickly and efficiently. A sawmill was constructed and put into operation, being run on a mutual basis—the first cooperative industrial plant in the United States. Since running the mill was then a relatively inexpensive affair, cut lumber could be supplied at rates lower than the average.

There were no elected officials in the community. No one had any more authority than anyone else. The only rule was voluntary participation. Individual freedom of action was the goal of the settlers; each man was to be his own lawmaker for himself only. As Warren wrote about the community later:

Harmonious society can be erected on no other grounds than the strictest individuality of interests and responsibilities. . . . Never shall any man know liberty until each and every individual is acknowledged to be the only *legitimate sovereign of his or her own person and property, each living and acting at his own cost*; and not until we live in a society where each can exercise this inalienable right of sovereignty at all times without clashing with, or violating that of others. This is impracticable just in proportion as we or our interests are *united or combined with others.* The only ground upon which man can know liberty is that of disconnection, disunion, individuality.[3]

The Village of Equity was successful and began to prosper. But the Warrenites were not as good ecologists as they were political and social philosophers. The cooperative's property was so close to the river and in such low land that it was fertile breeding ground for mosquitoes, and malaria quickly spread through the settlement. It became such a serious hazard that within a short time the experiment had to be abandoned with only inconclusive results.

Josiah Warren was not yet through with his practical demonstrations. He retired for a while to think and write, but on March 22, 1842, he opened another Time Store in New Harmony and operated it until 1844. Cost and price still obsessed him. The fact that price was determined by what the object would bring on the market was disgusting to Warren. It was "the pitfall of the working classes." To the capitalists, he posed a bitter question: "What is the price of a loaf of bread to a starving man?"

In *True Civilization,* published near the end of his life in 1869, Warren clearly discussed these issues. The motto of the Time Store, and of the labor-for-labor philosophy in general, might well be, "Cost—the limit of price." Cost was defined as "the endurance of whatever is disagreeable. Fatigue of mind or body is Cost. Responsibility which causes anxiety is Cost. To have our time or attention taken up against our preference—to make a sacrifice of any kind—a feeling of mortification—painful suspense—fear—suffering or enduring anything against our inclination is Cost."[4]

Returning to the idea of corn as the basis for a system of exchange, Warren made a sophisticated addition: Corn would be the unit by which all other labor was to be measured. If ten pounds of corn is the average product of an hour's labor, then any other labor as "costly" as the raising of corn would also be rated at ten pounds per hour. The still-unsolved question is just how "cost" in Warren's sense could be determined.

An equitable determination was arrived at, because in the New Harmony Time Store the labor note included a qualification relating to the intensity of work and the laborer's previous training. The arrangement was typically anarchistic—each person was to determine the value of his own labor notes. The anarchist's faith in the goodness of his fellow men is reflected here. But Warren had a practical safeguard for the system. If members of the cooperative did not agree with a man's evaluation of his labor they were perfectly free to refuse to trade with him or to honor his labor notes.

After two years Warren lost interest in the store, and even though it was successful, he closed it. Again, his restlessness was apparent. Three years later, in February of 1847, he opened yet another Time Store, selling his interest in it in April after only two months of operation. That same month, Warren's first book, *Equitable Commerce*, was published. It was the first native anarchist document to be published in the United States and the most popular of all the individualist antistatist's works.

The book was a formal statement of all that had been learned by the experiments with economics and society. "Society can never know peace until its members have liberty! but it can never be realized under any organization of society known to us."

A sample of Warren's Equitable money

Liberty is individual sovereignty over person and property. Law, always changing, is responsible for most crime because crime is a result of the very instability and insecurity caused by law.

In *Equitable Commerce*, one is reminded of the conservatism and agrarian bias of the early New England intellectuals. The only way to establish a self-sufficient society is described as a decentralization of manufactures and a limiting of products made to the local needs of the community in which the manufacture takes place. Always the empiricist, Warren also included, for the benefit of those who were interested, a set of instructions on how to start an equitist village.

He may then have decided it was time to follow his own prescriptions. In late summer or early fall Warren established, this time along the banks of the Ohio River, the community of Utopia. The settlement, of course, was based on the exchange of labor. It had its own brickyard, quarry, and other manufacturing operations. Warren set up a printing press and once more began to issue the *Peaceful Revolutionist*.

In his periodical, the founder spoke proudly of his new community. "Not one meeting for legislation has taken place. No organization, no delegated power, no constitution, no laws or by-laws, rules or regulations, but such as each individual makes for himself and his own business; no officers, no priests, nor prophets have been resorted to; nothing of this kind has been in demand. We have had a few meetings, but they were for friendly conversation, for music, dancing, or some other social and pleasant pastime. Not even a single lecture upon the principles upon which we were acting has been given on the premises!"[5]

Perhaps it is not always wise to trust a father's picture of his child, but Warren's enthusiasm was borne out by one of the colonists, E. G. Cubberley. "The labor notes put us into a reciprocating society—the result was in two years twelve families found themselves with homes who never owned them before. . . . Labor capital did it. I built a brick cottage one and a half stories high and all the money I paid out was $9.81—all the rest was effected by exchanging labor for labor. Mr. Warren is right, and the way to get back as much labor as we give is by the labor-cost prices—

money prices, with no principles to guide [them], have always deceived us."[6]

Following his usual pattern, once things began to go smoothly, Warren lost interest in the operations. Perhaps he thought it was his duty to move on to start other experiments. At any rate, he left the community after about a year. Whether Warren was conscious of the fact or not, this was one of the best and most significant tests he could have used on his theories. Most of the other Utopian communities in the United States, if they did not founder within a year or so, fell to pieces on the death or removal of the founder or leading figure. Utopia flourished. In a few years, the value of the labor note—though still subject to personal evaluation—was established: 20 pounds of corn an hour, a bushel of wheat for 6 hours of labor; 10 minutes of work for every quart of milk, and 20 minutes per dozen eggs; to make a pair of shoes was worth 3 to 9 hours of labor, depending on the quality and materials, and a pair of boots cost 18 hours.

By 1852, Utopia was a thriving community of about a hundred. It was expanded even further two years later, then having two Time Stores, a sawmill, a gristmill, a carpenter shop, three carpenters, two shoemakers, a glazier, and a painter—even anarchism had succumbed to the specialization of labor. Utopia continued as an anarchist, equitist community for about twenty-five years.[7]

Warren returned to Boston in 1848, where he associated with a small group of other antistatists. Although he had started his work alone, he now had a few passionately committed comrades who adhered to the same principles. Among the most notable were William B. Greene and Stephen Pearl Andrews—Warren's first major converts to his theories. Talk and conversation were not enough for Warren, however. Unlike the others, who were content to use language—often of a violent nature—alone, being anarchists only in words, he had once more to enter the field of practical sociology. In 1850, with the cooperation of Stephen Pearl Andrews, the community of Modern Times was established on Long Island, New York. This was Warren's first concession to the growing urban orientation of the United States. Long Island was near New York City, on which the settlement could depend until it was self-supporting. Moreover, the two men had friends and potential business contacts in New York who could facilitate the establishment of Modern Times. In January of 1851, Warren and a few others settled on the site, and on March 21, on about seven hundred and fifty acres of land only forty miles from New York City, Modern Times was officially begun. By the middle of 1853, the town was built; its quiet streets were made up of well-built, pretty cottages, again constructed on the labor-exchange principle, and tree-lined, clean and pleasant walks. In the spring and summer the strawberry beds and well-kept gardens made the community a lovely place.

Again, the anarchist settlement was able to function well with no official government or lawmaking body. The life was harmonious and congenial: "Mind Your Own Business," was the group's only law. Perhaps the presence in Modern Times of its founder had something to do with its peace and tranquillity. The American clergyman Moncure D. Conway visited the community in 1859 and met Warren.

There entered presently a man to whom all showed profound respect, and who was introduced as the reformer to embody whose ideas the village had been established. He was a short, thickset man, about 50 years of age, with a bright, restless blue eye, and somewhat restless, too, in his movements. His forehead was large, descending to a good full brow; his lower face, particularly the mouth, was not of equal strength, but indicated a mild enthusiasm. He was fluent, eager, and entirely absorbed in his social ideas. It was pleasant to listen to him, for he was by no means one of those reformers who, having fought with the world, hate it with a genuine philanthropic animosity, but one who had never been of the world at all, had never been stirred by its sins nor moved by its fears—one who was not deluged with negation, but amused with a troop of novel thoughts and fancies, which to him were controlling convictions.[8]

The New England atmosphere apparently had a strong effect on the group. Instead of the aggressive anti-intellectualism of the Utopia community, with its lack of lectures, Modern Times had weekly Parlour Conversations, informal discussions in small groups in which antistatist ideas were thoroughly explored. Beginning in 1854, Warren issued a monthly *Periodical Letter* (continuing until 1858), that explained his and the colony's philosophy and affairs. Apparently for the first time, Warren felt that some apologia was needed, for Modern Times was being vigorously attacked by many.

The economic and social views of the colonists were inflammatory enough. Added to this were the revolutionary sexual practices: men and women lived together without having been married—since the marriage contract as well as any other social or economic arrangement should be voluntary and not bound or restricted by law. Some of the women were ardent feminists and further offended the conservatives by wearing bloomers and men's clothes.

Eventually, sightseers came to stare at the queer inhabitants; papers devoted whole columns to the riotous life at Modern Times; and all sorts of eccentrics and mystics tried to enroll in the group. The basic aim of equitable and individualist living seemed to get lost. While the community survived for about twenty years, it never really flowered as Utopia had.

Another disturbing influence affected Warren, this time one with which he could not cope. He was keenly aware of the struggle against slavery that was being waged throughout the country. But life at Modern Times was somewhat isolated, and his distance from the more active urban places may have left him unprepared for the bitterness of the struggle. Warren was opposed to Negro slavery, which he considered but one of the many aspects of "wage slavery," but unlike almost all the other individualist anarchists in the United States he was not an ardent abolitionist, nor did he campaign actively against slavery.

Because of this, the Civil War, when it came, not only disrupted the life of Modern Times, but it also was a staggering blow to Warren. He could not reconcile himself to the war itself or its effect on the community. After he returned to Boston in 1863, he was even more confused. One of his elementary principles had been that armies and militarism with no exceptions were oppressors of individual freedom. But here, with a country at war, with civil unrest all around him, the practical element of his nature forced the antistatist to accept the strength of the State. He had to concede, at least on a temporary basis, that there was a need for armies, that battles had to be fought, and that order had to be maintained.

Although he continued to write, Warren never again tried to test his theories in any practical way. The one great failure of his ideas when they were tested by the Civil War may have made him afraid to experiment further. And the country itself was apathetic. The economic problems the war had created were enormous; any further attempts at setting up a Utopian community simply were not feasible.

In 1869, five years before his death, Warren published his last book. Even the title was an indication of his still-active concern with political structures. It was called *True Civilization: A Subject of Vital and Serious Interest to All People; but Most Immediately to Men and Women of Labor and Sorrow*. In the book, Warren made conclusive his opposition to government and law. But beyond this, he faced the proponents of communism and socialism with the antagonism of an archconservative, a stand typical of the individualist anarchists. He formally connected himself with the right rather than the left: "What is called conservatism has all the time been extremely right in its objections to communism and in insisting on *individual* ownership and *individual* responsibilities: both of which communism annihilates; conservatism has also shown wisdom in its aversion to sudden and great changes, for none have been devised that contained the element of success."[9] The communists, he said, "like moths flitting round a lamp, seem to learn nothing from their hurt, disabled, and prostrate companions, and never know that the flame can kill till it is too late to profit by the knowledge."[10]

Ironically, Soviet collective farms use a principle of payment similar to Warren's ideas. There, work is rated by the *labor day*, which varies with the skill needed to perform a job. Thus a tractor driver may be given three to five days' credit for one day's work, while a potato picker may spend the same amount of time on his job and be given credit only for half a day's labor. Each person on the collective has to put in a certain number of labor days each month. At the end of the month the total number of labor days of all the workers is divided into the net income of the farm, and each person is given his share of the profits, determined by his labor days for the month.

After *True Civilization* Warren suffered from ill health and lived with friends in Princeton and later in Boston, where he died after a long illness in 1874.

The field of action was left to his disciples—Greene, Andrews, Lysander Spooner, and Joshua K. Ingalls. These men determined that the next step in advancing anarchism in America was to bring the case to the people, to indoctrinate them in the principles of anti-authoritarianism. Two societies, the New England Labor Reform League and the American Labor Reform League, were founded as a means of spreading individualist antistatist thought. Although Warren was himself no longer active the last few years, he did belong to the groups.

Never again was there a man with the initiative, courage, and stubborn energy to undertake substantial testing of the basic doctrines of individualist anarchism. Warren's practical innovations eventually died out. But his philosophical work, which had anticipated that of Proudhon, had a great indirect influence on labor and currency reform in the United States.

7

Interlude: Some New
Influences on Individualist Anarchism

Native anarchism had been formed under the same influences that shaped the making of America, but by the middle of the nineteenth century, North America was no longer so isolated from Europe, and all thought—including anarchism—in the United States began to be influenced by European philosophers.

The 1840's was a particularly fertile decade in which almost all the political thought of the century had its origins.

One of the most powerful influences on American anarchism was that of the French mutualist Pierre Joseph Proudhon, (1809–1865), who once called himself a "man of paradoxes." Proudhon, a brilliant student, came from an extraordinarily poor family. One day, after winning a prize at school, he came home with the news to find that the family had no food. His earnings were needed to save them all from starvation, and the boy left his studies to become a proofreader.

In 1840, Proudhon published *Qu'est-ce que la propriété?* (What is Property?), a question he answered in the book with the statement, "Property is theft." In this work he advocated the formation of an anarchist society. Contrary to the implications of his statement, Proudhon was not a communist-anarchist. The property he called theft was only that which was earned without labor. Instead of dispossessing owners of land, houses, mines, and industries, he suggested that capital no longer be allowed to accumulate interest, thus limiting the extent of any man's fortune since excess capital would soon be eaten up by the needs of succeeding generations for food, clothing, lodgings, and so on.

Proudhon's major contribution was his invention of the mutual bank. This organization was to be based on the mutual confidence

PIERRE JOSEPH
PROUDHON

Culver Pictures Inc.

(voluntary participation) of all those who took part in the production of goods. Through the bank, these persons would be able to exchange products at cost value by means of labor checks that would represent the hours of labor needed to produce the merchandise in question. This, of course, was an idea quite similar to Josiah Warren's, but unique in that Proudhon theoretically established a bank as the medium through which the exchange was to be made.

The bank had certain advantages over the Time Store. For example, money could be lent without interest, but with a surcharge of about 1 per cent to cover administrative costs. In this way, Proudhon explained with romantic fervor, since everyone would be able to borrow the money required to buy a house, nobody would agree to pay any more yearly rent for the use of it. The same reason would eliminate mines, factories, private-

or State-owned transportation systems, and every other "thieving" institution. Once mutualism was established, the State would no longer be necessary because all the major relations among citizens would be based on voluntary agreement and regulated by account keeping. The State itself he called "that fictitious being, without intelligence, without passion, without morality."[1] This was a formulation similar to Warren's idea of the State as a purely linguistic construct. To replace the State, Proudhon advocated federalism, an interior and voluntary distribution throughout society of sovereignty and government. The twentieth century, he predicted, would be an age of federations. Proudhon's ideas directly influenced American economic thought, particularly that of the Populist movement of the 1890's which arose out of the discontent of farmers in the Middle West and West with the currency system.

At the time Proudhon was writing and until 1848, the hopes of the liberals and radicals throughout the world were centered on France. That country had suffered through a revolution far more bloody and bitter than that of the United States, only to have the revolutionary Republic overthrown. A series of unsuccessful governments followed, alternating between monarchy and republic. In 1848, the monarchy, under Louis Philippe, was again overthrown, and in February a provisional republican government was established.

But the workers were dissatisfied with the new government and determined to show their opposition to what they regarded as a deliberate violation by the government of their promised right to work. The unemployment problem was only aggravated by the February revolution. Finally, in June, the workers, led by radicals, began an unsuccessful uprising. It was ruthlessly suppressed, and the only effect it had was to show the French conservatives that they had been right to fear the workers and the socialists. Completely alarmed, the middle and upper classes now banded together; many of the liberties only recently received were taken away; new censorship of the press was introduced; and working hours were again made longer. Alphonse Lamartine, the poet and politician, said, "The Republic is dead." His melancholy assessment of the situation was echoed by visionaries all over the world who were bitterly disappointed by the split between the classes and by the unhappy results of the workers' protest.

In the United States a loosely knit group of Proudhonian anarchists, known as the Forty-Eighters, was formed of native Americans who had traveled in France, as well as of Frenchmen and of Germans who, many for political reasons, had settled for a period of time in America. For the most part, these men were completely unaware of the similarity between their beliefs and those of Josiah Warren.

Among the Americans in the group were William B. Greene and Charles A. Dana. The outstanding French member was Eliseé Reclus, who, along with Kropotkin, was the originator of anarcho-communism. Reclus lived in New Orleans for a time and traveled through the Middle West and East during 1853–1856. He met a number of sympathizers and was a persuasive spokesman for his beliefs. Among the Germans was Carl Heinzen, who came to the United States in 1848 in order to escape arrest in Germany. Although he returned to Europe for a short time, Heinzen came back and settled in New York in 1850 where he was an active campaigner for the emancipation of women, the abolition of slavery, and the immediate creation of a government directly responsible to the people.

These Europeans were the first of a growing group of foreign anarchists to arrive in the United States and preach a doctrine of anarchism that was progressively less in sympathy with that of the native American individualists. As the differences between the two groups became more pronounced, their mutual influence on one another weakened until soon the two factions were hostile to one another.

However, two Englishmen who were never antistatists, John Stuart Mill (1806–1873) and Herbert Spencer (1820–1903), and one German, Max Stirner (1806–1856), through their writings had a profound effect on the development of individualist anarchism. Mill, a noted economist and philosopher, like the American antistatists, was concerned with bringing economics into a relationship with morality and ethics. He wrote:

The things are there . . . mankind individually or collectively can do with them as they please, and on whatever terms. . . . Even what a person has produced by his individual toil, unaided by anyone, he cannot keep, unless by the permission of society. Not only can society take it from him, but individuals could and would take it from him if society did not . . . employ and pay people for the purpose of preventing him from being disturbed in his position. The distribution of wealth, therefore, depends on the laws and customs of society.[2]

Mill then pointed out that no economic system could arbitrarily be justified as the correct one. Economists could, on the basis of their social and moral philosophies, argue that men deserved a certain payment or a certain income for labor or capital, but their appeal had to be to social structure and to ethics rather than to an arithmetical calculation.

Spencer was frequently cited by individualist anarchists as one of their teachers. Essentially self-educated, he worked for a number of years as a railway engineer. Spencer's position was

JOHN STUART MILL

The New York Public Library

that of the philosopher of the scientific revolution of the late nineteenth century. As a friend of Darwin and Huxley, he was an evolutionist and attempted to trace the course of progress from the primitive to the more sophisticated and better throughout the history of the universe.

Spencer's ethical arguments developed from the idea that "the greatest happiness is the purpose of creation." So, good conduct is that which leads toward a pleasurable life in a society in which each man can pursue his own happiness without interfering with the happiness of others. In his first major work, *Social Statics,* published in 1850, Spencer included a chapter titled "The Right to Ignore the State." In it he put his argument that man had the moral right to withdraw from the State, refusing to pay taxes to it and doing without its protection. "Government," he wrote, "is essentially immoral . . . as civilization advances [so] does government decay. To the bad it is essential; to the good, not. . . . Magisterial force is the sequence of social rule, and the policeman is but the complement of the criminal. Therefore, it is that we call government a necessary evil."[3] To the American individualist anarchists, with their emphasis on scientific approach and on evolution, Spencer's philosophy supplied a justification for their views.

One of the most fiery writers of his time, Max Stirner was in reality a mild-mannered German schoolteacher whose real name was Johann Kaspar Schmidt. Always personally unassuming, of medium height, with white, slender hands, Stirner was a delicate and shy man. He was born in Bayreuth, and during his studies there and later at Berlin University where he was preparing himself for a teaching career, he was a serious and industrious pupil. But his studies were interrupted by the mental illness of his mother, whom he returned home to care for. Stirner's adult life was notably unhappy. After his mother's death, the young man married a girl who lived only a few years after they were married. His second marriage was unhappy and lasted just three or four years. Afterward, he was twice put into prison for nonpayment of debts.

From 1839 to 1844, Stirner taught in a private girls' school in Berlin. It was while he was in this quiet, sedate atmosphere that he wrote his revolutionary *The Ego and His Own*, published in 1845. In the book he rejects all moral and political ties and praises crime as an egoistic antisocial force. There is no "ought to be" for him; men are what they are. Various passages attack right, virtue, the State, law, God, country, family, and truth. Instead of all these, Stirner sets up one supreme law—self-welfare, or egoism.

"From the moment when he catches sight of the light of the world a man seeks to find out *himself*, and get hold of *himself* out of its confusion. . . . Accordingly, because each thing *cares for itself* and at the same time comes into constant collision with other things, the combat of self-assertion is inavoidable."[4] The ideal man is the egoist who wins in the conflict with society and other individuals, operating successfully in accordance with his own needs and happiness.

The egoist can then feel free to form a union with other egoists, with no rules or laws but simply for the common convenience.

You bring into a union your whole power, your competence, and *make yourself count;* in a society you are *employed,* with your working power; in the former you live egotistically, in the latter humanly, that is, religiously, as a "member in the body of the Lord"; to a society you owe what you have and are in duty bound to it, are possessed by "social duties"; a union you utilize and give it up undutifully and unfaithfully when you see no way to use it further. If a society is more than you, then it is more to you than yourself.[5]

What of the property of the egoist and of the union?

What then is *my* property? Nothing but what is in my power! To what property am I entitled? To every property to which I *empower* myself. I give myself the right of property in taking property to myself or giving myself the proprietor's power. . . . Let me say to myself, what my might reaches to is my property; and let me expand my actual property as far as I . . . empower myself to take.[6]

The other egoists, however, would have the same concept of property. Thus in the union the egoist protects his own property and can always withdraw from the voluntary association if it is threatened and he feels he cannot protect it.

For Stirner life is one continual amoral battle of force against force. The only good is the achievement of one's own "oneness," or uniqueness.

Stirner's ideas were spread in England and the United States by the anarchist John Henry Mackay, who considered him to be the spiritual father of individualist anarchism. Especially susceptible to Stirner's "egoism" and "selfishness" were the last great American native antistatist, Benjamin Tucker, and his circle.

8

Some Smaller Voices

A number of Americans advocated resistance on specific issues, such as slavery, and at times—without becoming anarchists themselves—approached the antistatist position. William Ellery Channing (1780–1842) was one of the inheritors of the Puritan tradition of separatism. While he himself was never an avowed antistatist—in fact he considered it the citizen's duty to respect secular government—his ideas are a logical foundation for the no-government philosophical structure of Christian anarchism.

Channing focused his attention on the individual's relationship to his God. He considered that the soul was responsible to itself and to God, but to no other constituted authority. No religious doctrine obtains; rather, it is for the individual to seek the truth and, once he finds it, to be faithful to it. He found that his views were in conflict with the doctrine of his religion, and in 1819 he delivered a sermon, "The Moral Argument Against Calvinism." In it he listed three principles that led to the schism within Protestantism that was finally resolved only by the establishment of the Unitarian Church. These three principles were: God is good; Man is essentially virtuous and his nature is perfectible; and man has free will, which includes the responsibility to act morally.

Channing held the same position on slavery as did the anarchists—he was opposed to it and to the annexation of Texas, which was thought to be a step that could only encourage the further spread of slavery in the United States. He had a passionate respect for liberty and for human nature. In his "Introductory Remarks" to a collected edition of his works he wrote:

It is because I have learned the essential equality of men before the common Father, that I cannot endure to see one man establishing his arbitrary will over another by fraud, or force, or wealth, or rank, or superstitious claims. It is because the human being has moral powers, because he carries a law in his own breast and was made to govern himself, that I cannot endure to see him taken out of his own hands and fashioned into a tool by another's avarice or pride. It is because I see in him a great nature, the divine image, and vast capacities, that I demand for him means of self-development, spheres for free action—that I call society not to fetter, but to aid his growth.[1]

These words are a call to revolutionary social reform. Channing could not but see that his own ideas were in conflict with those of any man who accepted the Constitution and the laws based on it. He developed a vision of a State whose political power would diminish continuously until it no longer existed. The only value government had was a negative one, to suppress injustice. If ever the laws of the State conflicted with higher justice, then, like Thoreau, Channing advocated civil disobedience and moral action instead. "The good of the individual is more important than the outward prosperity of the State."[2]

In political office he saw only evil, a maddened ambition, and in the concentration of economic or political power only a monstrous situation. "Human policy has almost always been in conflict with the great laws of social well-being, and the less we rely on it the better. The less of power given to man over man the better."[3] Channing was a pacifist, preaching his first antiwar sermon in 1812. His positions on all these issues were derived from that first anarchist work, Godwin's *Political Justice*.

That man would eventually arrive at a state of perfection led to a formal religious doctrine known as perfectionism, which ended as spiritual anarchism. Its founder was John Humphrey Noyes (1811–1886), a young Vermonter whose religious views were somewhat primitive and mystical. He began his argument with a Puritan text, "Be ye therefore perfect, even as your Father in heaven is perfect." In 1834 Noyes founded a monthly paper, the *Perfectionist*, and soon he had converted many notable abolitionists and radicals to his ideas; among the converts was the fiery orator and Christian anarchist William Lloyd Garrison.

Noyes believed that he and all those whom he converted were set free from law because they were saved from sin—an idea

JOHN HUMPHREY NOYES

Culver Pictures Inc.

much like that of Anne Hutchinson and the antinomians of early Massachusetts. From this basis, Noyes progressed to a view that all law was merely interference in the relationship between God and man. Here, St. Paul was his support: "Ye are not under the law, but under grace."

In a letter to Garrison in 1837, Noyes wrote:

> I have subscribed my name to an instrument similar to the Declaration of '76, renouncing all allegiance to the government of the United States, and asserting the title of Jesus Christ to the throne of the World. . . . I have renounced active co-operation with the oppressor on whose territories I live. . . . I must either consent to remain a slave till God removes the tyrant, or I must commence war upon him, by a declaration of independence and other weapons suitable to the character of a son of God.

Noyes then listed seven reasons why war should be made upon the State. And finally he said, "My hope of the millennium begins . . . AT THE OVERTHROW OF THIS NATION."[4]

Not content to proselytize by the written word alone, Noyes, like Warren, had to put his ideas to the test. So, under his guidance, the Utopian community of Oneida, New York, was founded in 1848. This settlement, which existed in the economic form of anarcho-communism, was perhaps the most successful Utopian attempt of the nineteenth century. The members vowed only their voluntary support to the group and only for so long as they chose to give it. Unfortunately, like Modern Times, this community received a certain amount of notoriety because of the sexual license of some of its members and because of Noyes's own belief in communal marriage.

The members of Oneida before their main building

Culver Pictures Inc

The Oneida settlement began with forty acres of land, which had been purchased for two thousand dollars, along with an old frame house, and an abandoned Indian hut and sawmill. The colonists had a chance to test the quality of their religion, for they were so poor for a time that the entire group had to sleep on the floor in the garret. The men and women were industrious, however, and Oneida prospered. They raised some fruit, made furniture for sale, sold cattle, and worked independently as farmers, blacksmiths, and at other trades. From 1857 to 1866, the two perfectionist communities—another had been established at Wallingford, Connecticut—did amazingly well, making a total net profit for the time of $180,580. By 1874, Oneida had 654 acres and 238 settlers, and it continued to prosper for a number of years.

William Lloyd Garrison (1805–1879), unlike the other individualist anarchists discussed so far, was not a descendant of a colonial family. His Irish mother had emigrated to the United States in the hope of finding a better life. She had been bitterly disappointed. Her English husband was a drunkard, who later

The inhabitants of Oneida in their dining room, from an article on "The Oneida Community of Free Lovers"

WILLIAM LLOYD
GARRISON

deserted his wife and three children. The family was unbearably poor. As a boy, William was apprenticed first to a cobbler and then to a carpenter. Unhappy at both trades, he was turned over to a printer, under whom he studied the craft for seven years. Garrison grew up to be that truly American phenomenon, the self-made man.

He early took part in the temperance movement, and then in 1828, under the influence of Benjamin Lundy, a Quaker friend, became an ardent abolitionist. At first, Garrison believed that the way to achieve his goals was through political action, but he soon took a more violent stand. By 1831, he decided that the only way to push abolition forward was to propagandize for it, so with no funds, no following, and only borrowed type, he began publication of *The Liberator*. The young man had just turned twenty-six. That he was arrogant and intolerant of views different from his own, even his best friends admitted; but he was also a brave, stubborn advocate of pacifism and of the abolition of slavery. He was lied about, hated, accused of the worst sins; nothing stopped him.

Eventually, his views reached their extreme ends. Garrison became a firm and aggressive perfectionist. Like Noyes, his only recourse was to declare war on the political State. First, he disenfranchised himself. Then he said the Constitution itself was unclean. His enemies, quite rightly, accused him of sedition. So opposed was he to the Fugitive Slave Law, requiring the return of slaves to their masters in the South after they had escaped to the North, that on July 4, 1854, he burned a copy of it. This was followed by a burning of the Constitution, which he called "a covenant with death and agreement with hell." Garrison threw it on the fire, let it burn to ashes, and then faced his audience with the cry: "So perish all compromises with tyranny!" Through his inability to accept just one law—involving the legality of slavery—Garrison had come into irreconcilable conflict with all law and the State.

Because he was also a pacifist, Garrison could not advocate the violent overthrow of either the institution of slavery or of the

A cartoon caricature of William Lloyd Garrison, 1835

government of the United States. He settled upon a doctrine of nonresistance and civil disobedience.

Pacifist ideas had interested American reformers as early as the first years of the nineteenth century. One of the first peace societies in the world had been founded in New York City in August of 1815, with David Low Dodge as its president. The nonresistants condemned both war and the use of any force either by individuals or by governments to enforce laws. They also took the stand that any laws contrary to Christian gospel should be disobeyed.

In 1837, Garrison and a number of his friends formed the New England Non-Resistant Society. In this group, Garrison formalized his antistatist position for the first time and denounced all law and government as being inconsistent with Christianity. The society officially came into existence on September 18, 1838, when the Declaration of the Society, written by Garrison, was issued.

The group visualized the eventual destruction of authority, and with it law and government. A new order was to emerge in which the individual would attain absolute freedom. His actions would be moral, guided by a love of God. The "scientific anarchists," such as Warren, Lysander Spooner, and William B. Greene, wanted to replace the laws of man with the laws of nature. This was not sufficient for the nonresistants, or indeed historically for any group of Christian anarchists. For these anti-statists, the laws of man are to be replaced by the laws of God as expressed in the Golden Rule and the Sermon on the Mount.

All of the nonresistants agreed on certain principles. Since they were opposed to government, they held it to be wrong to hold office or even to vote. The society itself took a stand against capital punishment, slavery, and war. The members were opposed to the idea of patriotism or to any national sentiments, believing rather that eventually all men would be brothers.

Opposition to the society, of course, was strong and vituperative. The group's publication, the *Non-Resistant*, lasted only three and a half years, until 1842, and the society itself only eleven years. By that time almost every nonresistant had had second thoughts.

Not only was public disapproval hard to bear, but the trend of the times and the almost sure approach of civil war led them to reconsider their stand. The Civil War presented an insoluble paradox to them. Although it was a war to which they were opposed as pacifists, it was a war against slavery, and they were abolitionists. With one exception they rejected their ideals or so seriously doubted them that they could not affirm them publicly. The one remaining faithful abolitionist pacifist of the society was Adin Ballou (1803–1890).

As a minister, Ballou found it necessary to assert his belief in both pacifism and the evils of slavery over any supposed claims to obedience that the government might have over him. A Christian's duty, he felt, is to disobey all temporal authority if by doing so he is following God's will. To Ballou, the nonresistants were forerunners of a time when governments of all kinds would be superseded by the "kingdom of Christ," a society in which man would fulfill his moral obligations to God.

ADIN BALLOU

Courtesy of The New-York Historical Society, New York City

The conclusion is therefore unavoidable that the *will of man* (human government) whether in one, a thousand, or many million, has no intrinsic authority—no moral supremacy—and no rightful claim to the allegiance of man. It has no original, inherent authority whatsoever over the conscience. . . . When [human] government *opposes* God's government it is *nothing;* when it *agrees* with his government it is *nothing;* and when it *discovers* a new item of duty—a new application of the general law of God—it is *nothing.*"[5]

Ballou eventually found himself too strongly in conflict with society. He retired to the country and cut himself off from everyone he knew.

There was yet another, even more extreme nonresistant—Henry C. Wright, the most forceful critic of government among the Christian anarchists. He stated flatly, "The powers assumed by all human governments to be essential to their existence and execution have been proved to be wrong; and the practices of such governments, without which they cannot exist, have been proved to be hostile to the spirit and positive commandments of Christianity. Therefore, human government is a wrong in itself."[6]

Born on a farm near Athol, Massachusetts, Lysander Spooner (1808–1887) had an odd beginning for a future anarchist: He studied law in Worcester, and later with Charles Allen, a noted law teacher of the time. It was said that Spooner knew the Constitution and constitutional law better than most other lawyers and judges in the country. He was also an able and clear writer, drawing on his knowledge to write the most devastating criticism of law ever attempted.

The event that triggered Spooner's anarchist sympathies involved a conflict between him and the United States Post Office. He was sure that the postal rate of twelve cents to send a letter from New York to Boston, and the charge of twenty-five cents for mail going from Boston to Washington, D.C., was outrageous. The reason for the high rate, he argued, was not the cost of the service but was because the government had a monopoly and could charge what it thought could be collected. To prove his point, in 1844 Spooner opened up a postal system of his own, the

American Letter Mail Company, which carried mail for five cents a letter. Spooner was successful, but the government, fearing that others would start their own systems too, soon closed him down.

In his criticism of the law Spooner attacked those who argued that government protects the rights of the people. Opposed to government is natural law, which is an expression of social custom. Man himself and alone is the best and only judge of what will be harmful and what helpful in his relations with his fellows. When at any stage of society government takes these flexible customs and makes of them a rigid code to be unflexibly obeyed, it freezes the organic development of the society at just that point. If government were really only an institution developed to protect the people, it would simply assure them of their rights to individual sovereignty, allowing the law of the people to be the law of the country. Instead of this, government and the State continually expand their authority to more areas of life and deepen what authority they already have. It seems that the only limitation to government is the endurance of the public. In his *Letter to Senator Bayard*, Spooner said, "Burn all the existing statute books of the United States, and then go home and content [yourself] with the exercise of only such rights and power as nature has given [you] in common with the rest of mankind."[7]

Without law, the binding factor of a free society would be individual integrity. "Each man has the right to acquire all he honestly can and to enjoy and dispose of all that he honestly acquires."[8] By extension, it is the individual's moral duty, if he lives honestly, to hurt no one and to give each other individual his due; the homeless, sick, weak, and ignorant must be cared for, but only voluntarily because it is a duty.

Recalling the typical individualist stand, Spooner envisioned a society of pre-industrial times in which small property owners gathered together voluntarily and were assured by their mutual honesty of full payment for their labor. Because each lived in accord with his own standards, a harmonious group life would be possible. This would be an aggregate of individuals living together in pursuit of their natural rights—life, liberty, property, and happiness. These rights were inalienable and could not be transferred. When the Constitution, which was based on a surrender of these rights to a central authority, was put into practice, it was a fraudulent document, and once men tried to force obedience to the laws based upon it, they were usurping the power of the individual.

Spooner, an ardent abolitionist, did not become an avowed anarchist until after the Civil War. After considerable thought he came to the conclusion that the war was based on the principle "that men may rightfully be compelled to submit to, and support, a government that they do not want; and that resistance, on their part, makes them traitors and criminals."[9] Although he agreed with the principle for which the war had been fought, Spooner could not accept what to him was a false premise, for if it was accepted as true, "the number of slaves, instead of having been diminished by the war, has been greatly increased; for a man, thus subjected to a government he does not want, is a slave."[10]

Continuing his case against authority and its representative government and law, Spooner stated that before the war it might have been possible to say that the government of the United States was free and rested on consent, but that it was impossible to say so now. If government rests on consent, it must be unanimous— the minority must agree with its actions as well as the powerful majority. There must be *the separate individual consent of every man who is required to contribute either by taxation or personal service to the support of the government.*"[11] It was a mockery then to claim any sort of unanimity of the government of the United States; the Civil War had been fought because of a great division between South and North over what constituted legal and moral behavior.

The final blow struck by Spooner was this: even if it might be argued that the Constitution was voluntarily and unanimously accepted by those who adopted it, they could only contract for themselves, not for the generations that came after them. Contract is the act of individuals, not of States.

Yet another leading anarchist was Stephen Pearl Andrews

STEPHEN PEARL ANDREWS

(1812–1886), born in Templeton, Massachusetts. The son of a Baptist minister, he studied law, but before practicing it taught in a ladies' seminary in Louisiana. Andrews was a brilliant scholar, learning Latin, Spanish, French, even Chinese (by himself in this instance, with only the aid of a textbook on the language). Eventually he knew thirty-two languages.

His phenomenal intellect was never satisfied. His interest in languages impelled him to a study of comparative philology, the science of language. He wrote a book on how to learn Chinese, two French textbooks, and a number of works on linguistic philosophy. After the death of his first wife, Andrews married a woman doctor who was also an ardent suffragette. In order to participate in her intellectual life and assist in her work he undertook the study of medicine at New York Medical College and received his degree.

One acquaintance wrote of him: "He impressed me as a type of pure intellect, by which I mean an intellect of abstract logical order; an unmalevolent Mephistopheles, for whose portrait indeed he might have sat, if into those quiet but alert features with their subtle leer of knowingness about the eyes, an artist could have touched the Mephistophelean scorn and malice which they lacked."[12] This was written not of Andrews in the prime of his manhood but of the older philosopher, nearly sixty, a dreamy, quiet, bearded member of the New York Liberal Club.

After the ladies' seminary, Andrews moved to Houston while Texas was still an independent republic and practiced law there. He grew more concerned with the lot of the Negro slaves and quickly became active in abolitionist circles. In 1843 he agitated against slavery so vigorously that his law practice was ruined and a mob destroyed his home. Andrews, his wife, and their newborn child had to flee the city. He still wanted to solve the problem of slavery. With a few friends he tried to get money from the English for the purchase of all slaves in Texas, who would be emancipated as soon as they were purchased. Before the project could be implemented, the war with Mexico made it impossible.

He and his family moved to the East, where, as mentioned earlier, he became a disciple of Josiah Warren, very active in the formation of Modern Times, although he never lived there.

In 1852 he published *The Science of Society*, which he considered to be his most lucid book on the subject of individualist anarchism. The first part was devoted to a demonstration of antistatism as a natural and final fruit of Protestantism, democracy, and socialism. In the second part, Andrews composed a theory of anarchism, especially its economic doctrine that cost should be the limit of price.

Along with Warren, Andrews was confident that the sovereignty of the individual was the most important single social goal. No two objects in the world were alike, and infinite diversity was an unchallenged law of nature. The more complex the object, the more elements it has and the more opportunities to differ from its kind. Man, being nature's most complex creature, is the most diverse form of life in the most ways. Therefore, any attempt to make a person conform to the standards of others thus perverts his potentialities. Andrews had demonstrated to his own satisfaction that individual sovereignty was as incontrovertible a natural law as Newton's laws of gravitation.

He never sought fame, but it was thrust upon him because of a series of letters written in 1853 in the form of a debate in which Henry James, Horace Greeley, and he took part. The letters were published in the New York *Tribune* and were enormously popular; they covered the subjects of love, marriage, and divorce. In one of the exchanges Andrews wrote:

> Give up . . . the search after the remedy for the evils of government in more government. The road lies just the other way—toward individuality and freedom from all government. . . . It is the inherent viciousness of the institute of government itself, never to be got rid of until our natural individuality of action and responsibility is restored. Nature made individuals, not nations; and while nations exist at all, the liberties of the individual must perish.[13]

Proudhon's influence on American individualist anarchism is best demonstrated in the career of William Bradford Greene (1819–1893). Born in Haverhill, Massachusetts, Greene was educated at West Point, served in the Army's campaign against the Seminoles in Florida, and then left the service to study for the ministry at Harvard Divinity School in 1842.

At the time he seemed to have a most promising future. A friend, Thomas Wentworth Higginson, said that he was "a young man who seemed to me the very handsomest and most distinguished-looking person I had ever seen; nor could anyone separate this picturesque aspect from his personality. He was more than six feet high, slender, and somewhat high-shouldered, but with an erectness brought from West Point. . . . His whole bearing was military and defiantly self-assertive. He had a mass of jet black hair and eyes that transfixed you with their penetration."[14] The handsome bachelor found an equally attractive wife, a Miss Shaw, who was quite lovely and almost as tall as he.

In 1845 after his graduation from Harvard, Greene served for a time as Unitarian minister in the town of West Brookfield, Massachusetts. Even at the beginning, however, his mind was not entirely with his congregation nor with the affairs of God. The young minister spent much of his time writing. At first the subjects were religious, but he soon turned to his first love—an odd interest for an ex-soldier and minister—problems of currency and banking.

He published *Mutual Banking* in 1850, the most thorough discussion of Proudhonian mutualism by an American. Greene noted that a bank existed only as a means of bringing borrowers and lenders together. It was only the instrument by which this mutual necessity was accomplished. The usual banks, because they charged interest on all loans and transactions were tools of the capitalists; they were guilty of making a profit beyond the proper payment for their labor. Also, the banks were uniquely free from the perils of laissez-faire capitalism that other industries suffered because the government guaranteed their rates of interest, no matter how many banks there were or what the demand for borrowed money might be.

Greene, drawing on a minor American tradition, suggested a mutualist land bank. One would join the bank by mortgaging any real property to it and receiving a bill of exchange worth just one-half of what the property was worth. All members of the bank honored bills of exchange presented to them by other members. Independent of Warren's work, Greene assigned a sum of about one per cent as the proper figure for the bank to add to the cost of the loan to cover its operating expenses. Land Banks had existed in the United States before. A successful one opened in Massachusetts in 1740 and operated quite well until the British Parliament passed an act dissolving it.

More than any other individualist antistatist, Greene advocated mutualism as the key issue in the struggle against the State. For him, freedom was fully significant only when it was united with a voluntary solidarity.

He was also an ardent fighter for women's rights. Before the Massachusetts Constitutional Convention in 1853 he made an impassioned plea for their cause. Later that year he went to Paris, where he met Proudhon, and lived there until the start of the Civil War. Like many other anarchists, for the war's duration he put aside his opposition to the State, returned to America, and joined the Union Army as colonel of the First Massachusetts Heavy Artillery; wounded in action or ill, Greene was discharged in October, 1862, and returned to Boston.

At the end of the Civil War the romantic philosophy and social criticism of the first half of the century lay in ruins. Not only did men have to face the poverty, destruction, and bitterness engendered by the struggle, but a new spirit was in the air as well. This time the war was not between the forces of liberalism and the old-fashioned imperialism of the slave owner; it was between the potentates of Eastern capitalism and the rising individualists of Western agrarianism.

With amazing rapidity systems of large-scale manufacture were set up, mining became a booming industry, and a transcontinental railway was soon to be a reality. A man could become a millionaire overnight, or within a few years, at any rate. The standards by which a man judged his life were changing, and with them his goals and ideals. Time was too short to worry about abstract theories of natural rights, or the necessity of local rule, or equality. As Vernon Parrington wrote, not only slavery was destroyed, but with it "the old ideal of decentralized democracies, of individual liberty." If they could get more money, men were willing to give the State more coercive powers; if industry would prosper, they were willing to concentrate authority in the hands of a few central figures. This was no longer the world of Thoreau, contemplating civilization at Walden Pond, but that of Commodore Vanderbilt.

Greene's career after the Civil War reflected the changed climate of the United States. He was less interested in mutual banking or theoretical propositions of anarchism. Instead he focused his attention on labor unions and worked with them in order to achieve a mutualistic society. When the First International was held (see p. 91), Greene was a member of the French section, again trying to find acceptance of his ideas among the laborers and trying to convince them that the issues involved in their struggle were not simply those of wages and hours.

One of Greene's colleagues in his labor reform work was Ezra

Heywood (1829–1893), who had first met Warren on his return to Boston in 1863. Like the other individualists, Heywood had been an abolitionist and had joined Garrison in his work in the late 1850's. Heywood's pacifism was of a somewhat more consistent nature than that of the other members of the groups.

After the Civil War, his attention was drawn to the unrest of the increasingly large numbers of industrial workers who were finding their conditions progressively worse. He decided that these men and women formed a perfect audience for ideas about a decentralized, anarchist economy. With Greene he led in the formation of the New England Labor Reform League in 1869. The two men introduced the League's *Declaration of Sentiments*, which not surprisingly was opposed to most of American society. For it, the League would substitute a country with "free contracts, free money, free markets, free transit, and free land— but discussion, petition, remonstrance, and the ballot, to establish these articles of faith as a common need and a common right. . . ."[15] The Declaration also advocated the removal of the tariff, free banking, and an economy based on labor notes. The League met twice a year for twenty-four years. From it originated the American Labor Reform League, which was founded in 1871 and led by anarchists until 1893.

Greene may have found the struggle in America too much for him. He left this country for England in 1873, staying there until his death in 1878. Heywood, on the other hand, continued to spread anarchist ideas in the United States. He greatly influenced the last significant individualist anarchist, Benjamin Tucker, who called him nothing more than an unterrified Jeffersonian democrat. Certainly the adjective "unterrified" was well chosen. Heywood continued to write—using strong and abusive language when he thought it was called for—on subjects that interested him.

After the railway strike of 1877, a particularly unpleasant confrontation of labor and management, the country was shocked to learn of the "Molly Maguires," a band of Irish-American radicals who were tried and convicted of murder. Most of the writers on the subject were sure that these men had gone too far, moving from radicalism to terrorism, and deserved to be executed. Heywood, however, insisted (probably without justification) that they had been convicted on the basis of weak and faulty evidence, that the Pinkerton men—the chief witnesses in the case—had perjured themselves and manufactured evidence because they had been ordered to do so by the railroad owners.

On November 3, 1877, while speaking in Boston, Heywood was arrested by Anthony Comstock, a social reformer who considered himself to be responsible for public morality and who had a quasi-official city position, and accused of sending obscene materials through the mails. He was later prosecuted twice more on the same charge. In one sense there was a certain basis to the accusation. Prudes and conservative Victorian gentlemen and ladies would certainly find certain articles in his periodical, *The Word*, offensive. In them he had advocated free love and sexual emancipation as part of the struggle for women's rights. On June 25, 1878, Heywood was sentenced to two years at hard labor. His conviction triggered a mass protest for his release and agitation for a repeal of the biased prudery of the Comstock Laws, devoted to the suppression of what Comstock and his followers considered to be obscene.

Heywood was released on December 19, 1879, and President Hayes issued a pardon for him the next day. But he was not yet finished with the courts. In the fall of 1881 and again in the spring of 1890 he was arrested and tried for the transmission of obscene materials. Although acquitted the first time, he had to serve another two years in prison after the 1890 trial; he was over seventy at the time and died only a little more than a year after his release from prison.

9

War Among the Radicals

As all sects of the radical movement began to focus their attention on the labor problem, conflicts among the factions was inevitable. In the early 1800's, it had seemed possible that anarchists, socialists, and communists could work together in the common struggle against exploitation and oppression of the working man.

As early as the 1840's, Proudhon had speculated on the possibilities of an international association of producers, and his followers were very prominent in the founding of the First International. There were several so-called Internationals. These were congresses of representatives from European countries and the United States who met to discuss the problems of the proletariat, or working class, and to develop a program of action to improve its lot.

In September of 1864, a group of Parisian artisans went to London and, with a group of their English colleagues, formed the International Working Men's Association. This first International was devoted to implementing and leading the direct economic struggle against capitalism. A number of Internationals met over the years; some of them were known by the color that identified their dominant group. Thus the Red International was primarily led by communists, and the Black International was a basically anarchistic meeting.

The founders of the First International were mutualists; these followers of Proudhon and Robert Owen were never of the individualist persuasion. Dominating the International were the socialists and communists; the anarchists—never a powerful faction in the executive—had to restrict themselves to attempts on the floor of the congresses to influence the course of the International's policy.

Losing more and more ground to the other radicals, the anarchists finally had to break with the International. This split occurred in 1872, during a congress battle between the Bakunists (anarcho-communists) and the Marxists. In that year, Ezra Heywood said, "It is not pleasant to see Dr. Marx and other leaders of this great and growing fraternity lean so strongly toward compulsory policies. If the International would succeed it must be true to its bottom idea—voluntary association in behalf of common humanity."[1]

After separating from the International, the anarchists decided that their only recourse was to form a totally anarchist international of their own. From 1872 to the Chicago Black International of 1881, they attempted to put this plan into operation. That it took nine years is due to their personal and theoretical opposition to any kind of central authority and their essential belief in small, autonomous local units.

The New York Public Library

A membership card for the International Working Men's Association

The Black International Congress was not a success. The anti-statists tried once more to return to their socialist comrades, and from 1889 to 1896 attempted to gain some sort of authority within the Socialist Second International, but they were ejected from the London Congress of 1896 and never again tried to join the socialists. From that time on, interrupted by the First World War, the anarchists made various sporadic attempts at forming an International of their own, but nothing was successful. Since World War II, no notable efforts have been made. And always, the anarchists involved have been anarcho-communists or syndicalists rather than individualists.

As soon as anarcho-communism had achieved some power in the United States, it was up to the individualists to evaluate their position on it and on all forms of mutualism. Regardless of whether the socialist or more extremist elements of the anarchists were opposed to the authoritarianism of the State and pledged to its downfall, it became clear that they were also opposed to the basic features of individualist anarchism. As early as 1849, William B. Greene had written, "In socialism, there is but one master, which is the State, but the State is not a living person, capable of suffering and happiness. Socialism benefits none but demagogues, and is emphatically the organization of universal misery. Socialism gives us but one class, a class of slaves."[2]

The very language used by anarcho-communists when they spoke of the class struggle, of worker against employer, was alien to the individualists. For the latter there could be no such thing as class; men were only individuals and owed allegiance to no one but themselves. Furthermore, no matter how loosely organized a collective might be, the very fact that there were no personal possessions, that all property was owned in common by the group, militated against egoism and seemed to be a fertile ground for the rebirth of some form of central authoritarianism that could only end once more in the formation of a State.

It is significant that the last major Congress attempting anarchist unity, the 1881 Black International of the International Working People's Association, was held in the United States at Chicago. Along with New York, Chicago was the major center for immigrant anarcho-communists, and the Black International was the first major demonstration of this type of antistatism in America.

From the time of the Forty-eighters, immigrants had been bringing mutualist and communist anarchism to America's shores. In the 1850's Wilhelm Weitling, a German, had atttempted to form a collectivistic anarchist community in Wisconsin, but the settlement failed. And a French immigrant, Joseph Dejacque, came to New York and began to issue an anarcho-communist periodical, *Le Libertaire*, in 1858. The magazine lasted only three years and is notable only because it was the first foreign-language anarchist periodical.

By 1880, however, the immigrant population in this country had increased significantly, and they came in larger numbers from eastern Europe, Germany, and southern Europe—the strongest areas of communist antistatism. Social Revolutionary clubs were started in New York, Chicago, and other cities. In October 1881, when the Black International met in Chicago, there were twenty-one delegates from fourteen cities in the East and Midwest. Most of these men were immigrants to America from Germany and Austro-Hungary. At the meeting the delegates declared themselves to be opposed to political action and in favor of the use of force to establish an anarcho-communist society. Prominent in the Congress were Albert Parsons, Michael Schwab, and August Spies, all later involved in the Haymarket Riot.

The power of anarcho-communism in the United States was increased enormously by the arrival in this country of Johann Most (1846–1906) in 1882. Most came to America directly from a sixteen-month jail term served in a London prison. He had been imprisoned because of an editorial he wrote in his periodical *Freiheit* (Freedom) asking that someone assassinate Tsar Alexander II. It had been Most's fifth time in jail.

He was a dedicated anarchist, convinced that a collectivist State with no government or law was the only possible salvation for mankind. His fanaticism may have been a necessary outgrowth of his terrible childhood. His unmarried mother had died when he was quite young, and when he moved to his

JOHANN MOST

From a rogue's gallery photo

The Bettmann Archive

father's home, his stepmother was not at all fond of him. To make things worse, the boy developed a disease that swelled one side of his face and disfigured him for life. When he was older, Most was able to grow a beard to hide the blemish, but as a boy it made him an object of ridicule. He said that his boyhood had been a nightmare.

Most was a good orator and a very persuasive writer. As soon as he arrived in the United States, a small, slender man whose hair was already graying, he set about reactivating *Freiheit,* and soon anarchists of his persuasion established equally revolutionary journals—among them Albert Parson's *Alarm* in Chicago, and *Truth* in San Francisco. Most also undertook a speaking tour of the country, giving lectures in every city where revolutionary groups existed. He tried to inflame men to action against the State by his advocacy of violence and "propaganda by deed." One of his works was a pamphlet entitled *Science of Revolutionary Warfare: A Manual of Instruction in the Use and Prepara-*

tion of Nitro-Glycerine and Dynamite, Gun-Cotton, Fulminating Mercury, Bombs, Fuses, Poisons, etc., etc. On May 5, 1883, Most published an article on dynamite in *Freiheit*, and in June told his readers how to manufacture nitroglycerine.

Certainly he was a master of inflammatory journalism:

> In giving dynamite to the downtrodden millions of the globe science has done its best work. The dear stuff can be carried in the pocket without danger, while it is a formidable weapon against any force of militia, police, or detectives that may want to stifle the cry for justice that goes forth from plundered slaves. It is something not very ornamental, but exceedingly useful. It can be used against persons and things. It is better to use it against the former than against bricks and masonry. . . . A pound of this stuff beats a bushel of ballots all hollow—and don't you forget it.[3]

Most was irresponsibly inciting men to violence, but he almost certainly didn't believe that he would be taken literally at his word. In fact, when Alexander Berkman, a Russian immigrant to the United States who was an anarcho-communist, attempted to assassinate the industrialist Henry Clay Frick in 1892, Most repudiated him and the action (which was an attempt at propaganda by deed).

Under Most's leadership, a Congress of the various European and American anarchist factions was called to meet in Pittsburgh on October 14, 1883. Twenty-six delegates were present. The majority of these men—with the exeception of Most, Parsons, and Spies—were not notable in the movement. The total membership of all groups represented at the Congress was minimal, probably only about five thousand, and most of these were from Chicago and New York. New York was Most's headquarters, and as such a definite center of the anarcho-communist movement. Chicago, because of its large numbers of German immigrants, many of whom were radicals of some variety, was also a fertile area for anarchist activity and propaganda; there was as well a long history of labor unrest in this Midwestern city.

At the Pittsburgh Congress, any possibility of union among the anarchists disappeared. It was clear at the outset that the anarcho-communists took it for granted that any political action or any strictly verbal propaganda would not be considered. The day before the Congress opened, Most had written, "It is only self-evident that the struggle of the proletariat against the bourgeoisie must have a violent revolutionary character, and the wage struggle alone will not lead us to our goal."[4] And again, the communist and syndicalist branches of the American anarchist movement themselves had trouble affiliating because they could not accept any central authority.

In its Manifesto, the Congress frequently referred to Jefferson, for example: "By force our ancestors liberated themselves from political oppression, by force their children will have to liberate themselves from economic bondage. 'It is, therefore, your right, it is your duty,' says Jefferson—'to arm.' "[5]

The Manifesto then listed the aims of the group:

First:—Destruction of the existing class rule, by all means, i.e., by energetic, relentless, revolutionary and international action.

Second:—Establishment of a free society based upon cooperative organization of production.

Third:—Free exchange of equivalent products by and between the productive organizations without commerce and profit mongery.

Fourth:—Organization of education on a secular, scientific, and equal basis for both sexes.

Fifth:—Equal rights for all without distinction of sex or race.

Sixth:—Regulation of all public affairs by free contracts . . . resting on a federalistic basis.[6]

While the Pittsburgh Manifesto is unclear, sometimes sloppily written, and indicates a hesitancy as to aims and the ways to achieve them, one thing it does show—a willingness to urge force and violence upon the workingmen as necessary factors in the class struggle. Although American labor had been willing when necessary to protect its actions and defend its members with guns and other weapons, it had always been a question of force to protect against force. This new idea, that armed workers should be prepared to strike out against the State—not with provocation, but as a revolutionary action—was imported from Europe and had never before had currency in this country.

But propaganda by deed had come to America, and in the

— 4 —

pots force is justifiable. because it is the only means, but they themselves have set the immemorial example.

By force our ancestors liberated themselves from political oppression, by force their children will have to liberate themselves from economic bondage "It is, therefore, your right, it is your duty " says Jefferson—"to arm!'"

What we would achieve is, therefore, plainly and simply

First.—Destruction of the existing class rule, by all means, i. e. by energetic, relentless, revolutionary and international action.

Second.—Establishment of a free society based upon co-operative organization of production.

Third.—Free exchange of equivalent products by and between the productive organizations without commerce and profit-mongery

Fourth.—Organization of education on a secular, scientific and equal basis for both sexes.

Fifth.—Equal rights for all without distinction to sex or race.

Sixth.—Regulation of all public affairs by free contracts between the autonomous (independent) communes and associations, resting on a federalistic basis.

Whoever agrees with this ideal let him grasp our outstretched brother hands!

Proletarians of all countries, unite'

Fellow-workmen, all we need for the achievement of this great end is ORGANIZATION and UNITY!

There exists now no great obstacle to that unity The work of peaceful education and revolutionary conspiracy well can and ought to run in parallel lines.

The day has come for solidarity Join our ranks! Let the drum beat defiantly the roll of battle. "Workmen of all countries unite! You have nothing to lose but your chains; you have a world to win!'"

Tremble, oppressors of the world' Not far beyond your purblind sight there dawns the scarlet and sable lights of the JUDGMENT DAY!

Issued by the Pittsburgh Congress of the "**International Working Peoples' Association**" on October 16th, 1883.

Published by the Bureau of Information.

International Working Peoples' Association,

107 Fifth Avenue, CHICAGO, ILLINOIS.

Subscribe for "**THE ALARM,**" a *Revolutionary Socialistic Newspaper*, devoted to the propaganda of ANARCHY. Published weekly at **No. 107 Fifth Ave., Chicago, Ills.** Sample copy free.

TO THE
Workingmen of America.

FELLOW-WORKMEN:—The Declaration of Independence says:

But when a long train of abuses and usurpations, pursuing invariably the same object, evinces a design to reduce them, (the people) under absolute Despotism, it is *their right, it is their duty* to throw off such government and provide new guards for their future security "

This thought of Thomas Jefferson was the justification for armed resistance by our forefathers, which gave birth to our Republic, and do not the necessities of our present time compel us to re-assert their declaration?

Fellow-Workmen, we ask you, to give us your attention for a few moments. We ask you to candidly read the following manifesto issued in your behalf; in the behalf of your wives and children; in behalf of humanity and progress

Our present society is founded on the exploitation of the propertyless class by the propertied. This exploitation is such that the propertied (cap'talists) buy the working force body and soul of the propertyless. for the price of the mere cost of existence (wages) and take for themselves. i. e. steal the amount of new values (products) which exceeds the price, whereby wages are made to represent the necessities instead of the earnings of the wage-laborer

As the non-possessing classes are forced by their poverty to offer for sale to the propertied their working forces, and as our present production on a grand scale enforces technical development with immense rapidity, so that by the application of an always decreasing number of human working force, an always increasing amount of products is created; so does the supply of working force increase constantly, while the demand therefor decreases. This is the reason why the workers compete more and more intensely in selling themselves, causing their wages to sink, or at least on

The New York Public Library

Part of an anarchist handbill issued by *The Alarm*, Parsons' magazine

three years that followed the Pittsburgh Congress, Most and his colleagues tried their best to convince the working men that force was their only way to achieve the goals they had set themselves. Americans, for the most part, did not take kindly to this "foreign" doctrine. They were appalled that such theories could be circulated in the United States; they were angry that the American way of life was being threatened; and they were afraid, because the labor movement had begun to show its teeth and the turmoil and revolution of the European class struggle might come to their country.

The impulse toward violence and armed resistance in Chicago was very strong. As early as 1875, an armed workingmen's organization had been formed in that city as a response to the oppression of striking workers; this group often drilled, as if to show the city its strength. Labor-management relations in Chicago had a long and bloody history. During a large strike in 1877, police brutality was notorious. At one point the police and state militia fought a mob of laborers at the Halstead Street viaduct on the South Side. Outnumbered by manpower and weapons, the strikers lost, and there were many dead and wounded on each side.

At the Pittsburgh Congress, the Chicago anarchists had been so dominant that the mixture of anarchism and syndicalism (a collectivist no-government society to be achieved through trade unions) that resulted was known as the "Chicago idea." The Chicago anarchists led in the founding of a Central Labor Union in 1884, which by 1886 had succeeded in recruiting more members than the more conservative and milder Amalgamated Assembly. The goals of the union were an eight-hour working day, a common labor front, and the open recognition of the class struggle. On one occasion, in October of 1885, the union adopted a resolution by Spies, which read in part: "Be it Resolved, That we urgently call upon the wage-earning class to arm itself in order to be able to put forth against their exploiters such an argument which alone can be effective: *Violence.* . . . Our war cry is 'Death to the foes of the human race.' "[7]

10

Dynamite Tonight

May 1, 1886, was a clear, fairly warm spring Saturday in Chicago. Ordinarily it would have been the start of another peaceful weekend. The men going to their jobs would have been thinking about sleeping late on Sunday, what they'd be having for dinner, or even the latest news of the famous Chicago baseball team, the White Stockings.

But this particular day, there was a feeling of fear and uneasiness throughout the whole city. Men stared at strangers, wondering if they were armed revolutionaries. Even that harmless-looking woman out for a walk with her baby could have bombs or guns in the carriage. Too many laborers were walking the streets as if it were a holiday; they should be at work. In fact, almost forty thousand workers were on strike for an eight-hour working day. Throughout that Saturday, neighborhoods witnessed small parades and street meetings with speakers haranguing their listeners in German, Polish, Bohemian, and English. Anticipating serious trouble, Chief of Police Ebersold had called out the whole police force and all the detectives, along with a number of special deputies and Pinkerton men.

The police had good reason to be afraid. Incitements to violence had multiplied over the last few years. In February of 1885, Parsons' periodical, *The Alarm,* with a circulation of about three thousand, had contained a "letter to the editor," by T. Lizius, an Indiana member of the International Working People's Association, that read in part:

Dynamite! Of all the good stuff, this is the stuff. Stuff several pounds of this sublime stuff into an inch pipe (gas or water-pipe), plug up both ends, insert a cap with a fuse attached, place this in the immediate neighborhood of a lot of rich loafers who live by the sweat of other people's brows, and light the fuse. A most cheerful and gratifying result will follow. . . . From thought to action is not far, and when the worker has seen the chains, he need but look a little closer to find near at hand the sledge, with which to shatter every link. The sledge is dynamite.[1]

Chicago's papers were not above turning the fear and unrest in the city to good advantage. On May 1, the Chicago *Mail* had an article with these paragraphs in it:

There are two dangerous ruffians at large in this city; two sneaking cowards who are trying to create trouble. One of them is named Parsons; the other is named Spies. Should trouble come they would be the first to skulk away from the scene of danger, . . . the first to shirk responsibility.

These two fellows have been at work fomenting disorder for the past ten years. They should have been driven out of the city long ago. They would not be tolerated in any other community on earth. . . .

Mark them for to-day. Keep them in view. Hold them personally responsible for any trouble that occurs. *Make an example of them if trouble does occur.*[2]

Dutifully, this is exactly what Chicago, and, indeed, the whole nation did, once trouble did occur.

May 1 came and went, and there was no violence; by evening the strikers on the streets seemed festive. That evening, a well-attended ball was the final event of the day. Sunday was more tense, but still peaceful. Few workmen left their families to meet anywhere in the city. Everyone was waiting.

At the end of two days without bloodshed, the police and strikers both relaxed. When Monday, May 3, came, it was clear that the eight-hour-day strike would spread. Workers in the building industry joined other strikers. Traffic was paralyzed on the Chicago River, at the freight yards, and for the most part at railroad stations. No work was done at the steel mills. This time the police began to act. The parades and meetings that were following the peaceful pattern of Saturday were not allowed to go on without obstruction. Policemen used clubs and threats of worse trouble to scatter the strikers.

Finally, unavoidably in that atmosphere, violence was set off.

August Spies, an anarchist who was one of the "two dangerous ruffians," had been asked to address some strikers on Monday afternoon. The site of the meeting was only a few blocks from Chicago's McCormick Harvester Works, where a lockout of fourteen hundred workers begun in February was still in force; for two months the factory had been operated by scabs, nonunion workers who refused to recognize the strike, and any formal meeting of McCormick strikers—with or without their wives and children—was broken up by policemen, some of them on horseback, wielding clubs.

In the middle of Spies's speech, the bell at the McCormick plant rang, a signal that the nonunion workers were finishing their shift. Already overconfident because of the last three days of labor solidarity, about five hundred men in Spies's audience— all of them locked-out McCormick workers—decided to race to the plant to heckle the homeward-bound scabs. Spies pleaded with them to come back, but without effect. The angry mob moved from heckling to an attack on the strike-breakers so fierce that it drove them back into the factory.

Only a few police were at the plant; because they were so outnumbered and frightened, without thinking they fired their revolvers into the crowd in an attempt to break it up. They were soon reinforced by a detachment of about two hundred armed police who used guns and clubs to quiet the strikers. Spies, who was still speaking, heard the shots and was told by a witness to the riot that many strikers had been killed.

Actually, one striker had died immediately, and five or six were seriously wounded; many others were less seriously hurt. The police had only six injuries and no deaths. But Spies, who trusted the report he heard, was convinced that many of the workers had been killed. He issued a circular calling the workingmen of the city to arms to avenge their dead comrades.

The Chicago newspapers again did what they could to fan the controversy. They first published erroneous reports claiming that six of the strikers had been killed. These were followed by stories claiming that the whole mob had been anarchists, that they were "liquor-crazed."

A meeting to protest the murder of the McCormick strikers was scheduled at the old Haymarket on Randolph Street for the next night, Tuesday, May 4. The calm of the first days of the work stoppage was gone. The city's laborers were in a bitter mood. Strikers were attacked by police throughout the day, and in retaliation a drug store whose phone had been used to call the police was completely demolished.

Spies, who had been asked to speak to the Haymarket meeting, discovered that the circular advertising it contained a call for armed men to come to the assembly; he refused to talk unless the request was omitted before the circular was distributed. So, only a few hundred of the twenty thousand handed out bore the deleted line.

It was still believed that the police would be able to control the city. Mayor Harrison gave permission for the meeting to begin at seven-thirty. The Haymarket, which was a wide opening in Randolph Street between Desplaines and Halstead, was in the heart of the meat-packing and lumber district. It had been chosen because it was supposed to be able to accommodate twenty thousand people. Only half a block away was the Desplaines Street police station, where a large squad was posted in case of trouble.

Only about twelve hundred persons had gathered by the time Spies reached the Haymarket. The workers were unorganized, gathered together in small knots of men, quietly talking together. After a good deal of hesitation and an attempt to reorganize the evening, Spies got up on top of a wagon in front of the Crane Brothers factory and addressed the crowd in German for about twenty minutes. He was a slight man, weighing about 150 pounds, with curly, thick brown hair and a mustache. He was a hesitant speaker, and his reluctance to say anything inflammatory was again clear. While the speech was a vigorous protest against McCormick and the other capitalists, it was not a cry for violent action.

Albert Parsons spoke next, demanding the eight-hour day at once; then Lancashire-born Samuel Fielden got up to talk to the men. It was about ten o'clock and clouds that had been gathering

The Black Flag of Anarchy

Attention Workingmen!

GREAT

MASS-MEETING

TO-NIGHT, at 7.30 o'clock,

AT THE

HAYMARKET, Randolph St., Bet. Desplaines and Halsted.

Good Speakers will be present to denounce the latest atrocious act of the police, the shooting of our fellow-workmen yesterday afternoon.

Workingmen Arm Yourselves and Appear in Full Force!

THE EXECUTIVE COMMITTEE

Achtung, Arbeiter!

Große

Maffen-Verfammlung

Heute Abend, ½8 Uhr, auf dem

Heumarkt, Randolph-Straße, zwischen Desplaines- u. Halsted-Str.

☞ Gute Redner werden den neuesten Schurkenstreich der Polizei, Wem fie geftern Nachmittag unfere Brüder erfchoß, geißeln,

☞ Arbeiter, bewaffnet Euch und erfcheint maffenhaft!

Das Executiv-Comite.

The handbill calling for the mass meeting at the Haymarket

all evening suddenly seemed even more menacing. Almost at once a heavy wind sprang up and a strong drizzle began. Within moments the small crowd began to disperse. Fielden went on with his speech: "People have been shot. Men, women, and children have not been spared by the capitalists. . . . You are called upon to defend yourselves, your lives, your futures. . . . Any animal, however loathsome, will resist when stepped upon. Are men less than snails and worms? I have some resistance in me; I know that you have, too."[3]

At about this point, Mayor Harrison visited the meeting and found it quiet and orderly. Only a few hundred men were left. He went to the Desplaines Street police station, talked with Captain John Bonfield, and after saying he was sure there would be no trouble, went home to bed.

Putting Captain Bonfield on duty that night had been an unfortunate choice. He was known throughout the city for his brutality and hatred of the workers. Only a few minutes after Mayor Harrison's visit, Bonfield and Captain Ward took 180 men to the Haymarket, stopping just a few feet from where Fielden was still speaking. He had just said, "In conclusion. . . ." The meeting was within seconds of being over. Neverthless, Captain Ward said, "In the name of the people of the state of Illinois, I command this meeting immediately and peaceably to disperse."

Fielden replied, "We are peaceful." But he, Spies, and the others started to get down from the wagon.[4]

At that instant, a dynamite bomb was thrown from somewhere near the speakers' wagon at the police, exploding just at the front of their ranks. Sixty-six police were wounded; one later died. For just a few seconds everyone stood frozen, amazed at what had happened, then the enraged police gathered together and attacked the workers, some of whom were armed, but most of whom were simply running away from the trouble. They fired wildly into the crowd, killing several and wounding many. Within a minute the only occupants of the Haymarket were the dead and wounded; the blood of the crowd and of the police mingled on the street.

To this day, no one knows who threw the bomb. It has been claimed by the two sides that the guilty were variously anarchists,

An artist's version of the Haymarket Riot

agitators in the pay of the Pinkerton organization, someone inspired by Captain Bonfield, an unaffiliated madman. Regardless of who was guilty, the hysteria that swept Chicago and the rest of the nation after the bombing was shocking. The anarchists were publicly blamed for it at once, and the newspapers demanded vengeance. Among other epithets, they were called Bloody Brutes, Red Ruffians, Bloody Monsters, and Bomb Makers in all the papers.

The *New York Times* headed its front-page May 5 story, "Anarchy's Red Hand." The story began:

The villanous teachings of the Anarchists bore bloody fruit in Chicago tonight, and before daylight at least a dozen stalwart police men will have laid down their lives as a tribute to the doctrine of Herr Johann Most. [After identifying all the labor meetings of the day as "anarchistic," the *Times* went on.] It should be borne in mind that

WHEN HIS SKIN IS NOT IN DANGER, AND—

WHEN IT IS

A cartoon deriding Most when he refused to act in the anarchists'
behalf after the Haymarket Riot

the men who were present at the Anarchist meeting were, with few exceptions, fellows with no visible support and professional agitators. They were not there to right any specific wrong, but to listen to wild harangues, such as they hear upon the lake front and in the Anarchist halls on Sunday. . . . Everything points to a preconceived plan on the part of Spies, Parsons, and Fielden to try the effect of one of their bombs.[5]

Everyone knew who the guilty were and what their fate should be. A trial hardly seemed necessary. The next day, the *Times* headlined the arrests of August Spies, Samuel Fielden, Michael Schwab, and Adolph Fischer, with the phrase "Crushing Anarchy." The men, as they sat in police headquarters, contrasted sharply with one another: the thin, handsome, thirty-five-year-old Spies; Schwab, fifty, tall, bony, with steel-rimmed spectacles; young Fischer tall, well-built, in his late twenties; and strong, broad-shouldered Samuel Fielden. The accused were soon joined by George Engel, Oscar Neebe, and Louis Lingg. Albert Parsons, the only native-born American in the group and probably the most important, was still at liberty. Strangely, Rudolph Schnaubelt, who was later accused as the actual bomb thrower, was arrested and released.

The arrests were in the hands of Captain Michael J. Schaack, a man who had a fertile imagination and—in his eagerness for political advancement—a great desire to make himself famous. Many anarchists were arrested and later released. Bombs were "found" all over the city; they probably did not exist at all or had been planted there by the police. In his book *Anarchy and Anarchists*, Schaack told tales of great plots he had uncovered just in time; of anonymous threats; of masked men and veiled ladies. All of these fabrications might have been laughed at at some other time. In Chicago, the police and public took them quite seriously. Verification for this comes not from a sympathizer with the anarchist position but from former Chief of Police Ebersold, who, in an 1889 interview published in the Chicago *Daily News* said:

It was my policy to quiet matters down as soon as possible after

AUGUST SPIES

ALBERT R. PARSONS

The three most famous
Haymarket defendants

Culver Pictures Inc.

SAMUEL FIELDEN

the 4th of May. . . . On the other hand, Captain Schaack wanted to keep things stirring. He wanted bombs to be found here, there, all around, everywhere. . . . Now here is something the public doesn't know. After we got the anarchist societies broken up, Schaack wanted to send out men to organize new societies right away. You see what this would do. He wanted to keep the thing boiling, keep himself prominent before the public.[6]

The police went at the business of breaking up the anarchist groups with fervor. They made an extended series of raids, often without warrants, breaking into and searching private homes, offices, and meeting halls.

The papers helped Chicagoans reach a peak of hatred and fear. On May 6, the Chicago *Herald* had in an article: "The rabble whom Spies and Fielden stimulated to murder are not Americans. They are offscourings of Europe who have sought these shores to abuse the hospitality and defy the authority of the country."[7] The element of foreignness both increased the public's fears and made it more anxious to exact severe punishment. In order to purify the city, the color red—the symbol of the revolution—was not allowed in Chicago street advertising.

On June 21, 1886, the seven men under arrest were tried for murder before Judge Joseph E. Gary. Albert Parsons was still missing and Rudolph Schnaubelt, once he had been released, vanished and was never found; but the two men were indicted along with the others. On the first afternoon, as agreed with his defense lawyers William Black and William Foster, Parsons surrendered himself in court. If he had not turned himself in, Parsons probably would not have been found, but he told a friend, "They will kill me, but I could not bear to be at liberty, knowing that my comrades were here and were to stand trial for something for which they were as innocent as I."

The basis of the group indictment was that the Haymarket bomb was the result of an anarchist conspiracy to which the men on trial were accessories, and that Schnaubelt had thrown the bomb. Judge Gary refused to allow the prisoners to have separate trials, so evidence against any one individual weighed against all eight.

Choosing the jury took twenty-one days. The special bailiff appointed by the court to select possible jurors said, "I am managing this case, and know what I am about. Those fellows are going to be hanged as certain as death. I am calling such men as the defendants will have to challenge peremptorily and waste their time and challenges. Then they will have to take such men as the prosecution wants."[8]

Judge Gary, along with almost all of the city of Chicago, had decided before the trial that the anarchists were guilty. He did all he could to see that the jury favored the prosecution, and his rulings on the defense challenges were almost wholly biased.

The prosecutor made it apparent from the outset that the facts of the case were less relevant than that the indicted were noted anarchists. His opening address began:

For the first time in the history of our country are people on trial for endeavoring to make anarchy the rule, and in that attempt for ruthlessly and awfully destroying life. I hope that while the youngest of us lives, this in memory will be the last and only time in our country when such a trial shall take place.... The preachings of Anarchy [by] ... these defendants hourly and daily for years, have been sapping our institutions, and ... where they have cried murder, bloodshed, Anarchy, and dynamite, they have meant what they said.[9]

The state attempted to prove that there was a "Monday night conspiracy," triggered by the publication of the word *Ruhe* (meaning "rest" and "sleep" as well as "gun rest") in the German-language anarchist paper *Arbeiter-Zeitung*, and that the publication of this word was the trigger to an uprising and the cue to the throwing of the Haymarket bomb. Certainly the word did appear in the paper, but there was no substantial evidence to indicate that it was a signal of any sort. The authenticity of the prosecution witnesses was questionable; one had been paid money by Captain Schaack, who also got him a job.

A witness by the name of Gilmer claimed that he saw Spies light the bomb and Schnaubelt throw it. But Gilmer's testimony as to where the bomb came from was contradicted by sixteen eyewitnesses; the rest of his statement was not supported by anyone else and was disputed by several of the eyewitnesses. Also, he was called a perennial liar by witnesses who knew him and had probably been paid by the prosecution.

The next governor of Illinois, John Peter Altgeld, reviewed the trial in connection with a possible pardon for some of the anarchists. His opinion of the testimony was: "Much of the evidence given at the trial was a pure fabrication; . . . some of the prominent police officials, in their zeal, not only terrorized ignorant men by throwing them into prison and threatening them with torture if they refused to swear to anything desired, . . . but they offered money and employment to those who would consent to do this."[10]

Louis Lingg, at twenty-two the youngest of the group, was a fanatical anarchist. He was accused of having made the fatal bomb. And he did make bombs and then allow others to take them. Yet no testimony proved that the Haymarket bomb was one of his. Lingg himself was not present at Haymarket Square that evening. Engel, too, had not been at the scene of the bomb throwing. A plain-faced, stolid German, he had been at home drinking beer with his wife and some friends. He stood accused only because he had been a member of the "Monday night conspiracy." Fischer, who had been at the scene earlier, had left before the bomb exploded. Only testimony linking him with the anarchist movement was presented as evidence against him. Thirty-six-year-old Neebe, a powerfully built tinsmith, was perhaps the most unfortunate of the accused. He was not particularly bright, nor had he been extremely well known in radical circles. His only crime seemed to be that he held two dollars' worth of stock in the *Arbeiter-Zeitung;* that he commented on the evening of May 3, "It's a shame that the police act that way, but maybe the time will come when it gives the other way—that they [the workers] get a chance, too";[11] that he had been in the *Arbeiter-Zeitung* office on May 5, and that he had two guns, a sword, and a red flag in his home.

There was extensive testimony that Spies, Fielden, and Parsons never left the wagon from which they spoke. And the evidence that Schnaubelt threw the bomb was scanty and almost totally discredited.

This was the prosecution's case that Grinnell began summing up for the jury on August 11. It had been told time and again in the courtroom that the men were anarchists and that some of them had written or spoken incitements to violence to a greater or lesser degree at some time or other. In fact this is all the state had managed to make clear. State's Attorney Grinnell charged the jury. "Law is upon trial. Anarchy is on trial. These men have been selected, picked out by the grand jury and indicted because they were leaders. They are no more guilty than the thousands who follow them. Gentlemen of the jury; convict these men, make examples of them; hang them and you save our institutions, our society."

On Thursday, August 19, the case went to the jury, which deliberated for three hours.

On the morning of the twentieth the defendants were brought into court and closely guarded. All eight were pale, uneasy, and exhausted. Then, at ten, the verdict was read. The result was as expected. Spies, Schwab, Fielden, Parsons, Fischer, Engel, and Lingg were sentenced to death; Neebe was sentenced to fifteen years in prison. The crowd waiting in front of the courthouse cheered at the news. One paper headlined the verdict, "Chicago, the Nation and the Civilized World Rejoice," another, "The Scaffold Waits—Seven Dangling Nooses for the Dynamite Fiends."

It seemed that not only were murderers going to be executed, but at the same time anarchism was dead in the United States. Americans could breathe freely, knowing that a democratic country would be their children's heritage. The communists, nihilists, few remaining anarchists, and socialists should take notice of their possible fate and slink out of a country that had shown itself brave enough to resist their cowardly attacks. This at least was the view taken by the majority and certainly almost every newspaper in the country. Only radical periodicals and papers sympathetic to the cause of labor were critical of the verdict.

Each of the defendants was given an opportunity to speak before Judge Gary passed sentence. Every one of them did so, some for hours, some for only a few minutes. Interest centered especially around what Parsons would say. Not only was he the sole native-born American, but his ancestry could be traced back

SHORT HOURS FOR ANARCHISTS -- HOIST THEM BY THEIR OWN PETARD.

Culver Pictures Inc.

An anti-anarchist newspaper cartoon, 1886

to the second *Mayflower* crossing of pilgrims; he had served in the Confederate Army for four years; and he had entered politics as a Republican.

Parsons, a short dark-haired man, was the best speaker of all the defendants. After lengthily outlining his views on the evils of capitalism and the history of labor in America, Parsons said, "dynamite comes as the emancipator of man from the domination and enslavement of his fellow men. . . . It is democratic; it makes everybody equal. . . . It is a peacemaker; it is man's best and lasting friend."[12]

Dynamite Tonight

All appeals for a retrial were denied. All attempts to win clemency from Governor Richard J. Oglesby were futile. On November 11, 1887, Lingg committed suicide in his cell with some sort of explosive device. The evening of his death the governor commuted Fielden and Schwab's death sentence to life imprisonment.

At about midnight that same night Spies, Parsons, Fischer, and Engel were simultaneously placed on the gallows. Fischer helped the man who was working on his noose to adjust it. Spies said his was too tight and asked that it be loosened. Hoods were placed on their heads. The four spoke one at a time, giving voice to their last words:

Spies: "There will come a time when our silence will be more powerful than the voices you strangle today!"

Fischer: "Hurray for anarchy—this is the happiest moment of my life!"

Engel: "Hurray for anarchy!"

Parsons: "Will I be allowed to speak, O men of America? Let me speak, Sheriff Matson! Let the voice of the people be heard! O—"[13]

The traps were sprung. The four were dead.

An anti-anarchist cartoon of 1889. Note that the sayings on the wall are the last words of the Chicago anarchists

But the case was not yet finished. In November of 1892, John Peter Altgeld was elected governor of Illinois. One of his first official acts was an announcement that he would review the Haymarket trial. After study he issued a statement declaring that the constitutional rights of the defendants had been violated, that the trial was unfair, that the evidence was in large measure perjured or improper. At the cost of an extremely promising political career, ruined by his decision, Altgeld pardoned absolutely Neebe, Schwab, and Fielden on June 16, 1893.

11

The Last Great Individualist: Benjamin Tucker

The Haymarket affair split radicals apart. Not only were the two factions of anarchists irretrievably separated, but a similar schism affected other radical movements. At the same time, a number of persons were converted to anarchism or some other libertarian philosophy by the Haymarket trial and executions. One of the more extreme examples is that of Voltarine de Cleyre, who had been named after the philosopher Voltaire.

She was born after the Civil War, on November 17, 1866, in Leslie, Michigan, and died in 1913, just prior to the First World War. Miss De Cleyre was so affected by the trial and execution of the Chicago anarchists that she immediately became an avowed antistatist. Her early life had been sheltered. At first contented with her quiet, bourgeois life, when sent to a convent in her teens she rebelled and ran away after only a few weeks.

Voltarine was shy and reserved. It was hard for people to get to know her, and she was most at ease with animals. Ignorance and stupidity infuriated her. Yet she seemed to be another person when she appeared on the lecture platform, dressed theatrically in a sort of toga with two long, full braids of hair; in her, anarchism had a noble advocate.

She looked upon antistatism as a search for order. "The conditions of life press upon me: I must do something with my brain. I cannot be content to regard the world as a mere jumble of happenings for me to wander my way through, as I would through the mazes of a department store, with no other thought than getting through it and getting out."[1]

She felt that the claims of the individualists to a scientific standpoint alienated them from humanity. "I think it has been the great mistake of our people, especially of our American anarchists represented by Benjamin R. Tucker, to disclaim sentiment. Humanity in the mass is nine parts feeling to one part thought; the so-called 'philosophical anarchists' have prided themselves on the exaggeration of the little tenth, and have chosen to speak rather contemptuously of the 'submerged' nine parts."[2]

When the Haymarket anarchists were arrested and the trial began, Tucker, as the leader of the individualists, made his position apparent at once in his periodical *Liberty*. He stated that he was unalterably opposed to the concept of propaganda by deed and to the entire type of anarchist philosophy as it was put forth by Johann Most.

In one editorial, Tucker wrote about the use of force: "But one thing can justify its exercise on any large scale; viz., the denial of free thought, free speech, and a free press. Even then its exercise would be unwise unless repression were enforced so stringently that all other means of throwing it off had become hopeless." The only means of accomplishing the social revolution, he went on, was "by means of agitation, investigation, experiment, and passive resistance. . . . The day of armed revolution is gone by. It is too easily put down."[3]

The threat of anarcho-communism as a competing ideology was not the only problem faced by individualist anarchists at the end of the nineteenth century. The frontier had advanced almost all the way across the country. The Midwest was being settled quickly, and as the pioneers moved to the Far West, their individualism and opposition to any exterior authority gave way to cooperation with the government and respect for its activities. Frontiersmen who settled down in towns discovered that a sheriff or marshal was needed to maintain law and order. Men made the transition from hunter to merchant, and merchants found they prospered most when aided by laws that assisted commerce.

In the South, within a few years after the Civil War, the artificial local governments that had been imposed on the Southern states during the Reconstruction collapsed. Authority became centralized in each state, and the idea of strong local self-rule no longer seemed workable.

The very act of settlement in the Western territories required different procedures than the Midwest had. In the arid areas, irrigation projects—of necessity cooperative and conducted under the paternal eye of the federal government—were the only possible way to make land habitable for agriculture.

That there would soon no longer be a frontier for dissenters to flee to, combined with the increasing complications in society created by the modern methods of manufacture and the lack of solidarity among the working class, made the intellectual climate of the United States unfavorable to individualist anarchism.

The individualists, too, had grown weaker. They combated a new spirit of materialism and a desire to "see how it would work" with activity restricted purely to thought and writing. The urge to test directly principles that had typified Warren's anarchism now no longer existed. Instead, the individualists surrendered to the cities and sat home wrestling with the huge modern problems of economics. They refused to fight in the public arena for the liberation of the masses as the other radicals of the time were doing.

Yet before individualist anarchism surrendered its stake in American political argument, for at least the next forty years one last great voice spoke out for it—that of Benjamin Tucker, the man who among all the individualists received the most sympathy and attention from the general public in the United States.

Tucker was born in South Dartmouth, Massachusetts, on April 17, 1854, just a few years before the Civil War. His father had been in the business of equipping whalers. When that industry disappeared, the elder Tucker turned to dealing in spices and groceries.

Young Benjamin was brought up in a well-read, socially conscious family. He was a bright child, and apparently was greatly affected by the ideas of William J. Potter, the Unitarian minister of the church his parents attended. The boy, like the man later on, was always cheerful, friendly, and kind. At an early age he was interested in social problems, and was, as he later said, "a daily devourer of the New York *Tribune* from the age of twelve." Benjamin read widely in his early teens: the evolutionary theories and modern science of Charles Darwin, Thomas Huxley, and

BENJAMIN TUCKER

John Tyndall; the economic theory of John Stuart Mill; and the social philosophy of Herbert Spencer. All this had a significant effect on his developing thoughts. Benjamin also at that time regularly attended lectures at the New Bedford Lyceum, where persuasive anarchist speakers such as Wendell Phillips and William Lloyd Garrison could be heard. Looking back on that somewhat solemn adolescence, Tucker said of it:

I naturally took a decided stand on all religious, scientific, political, and social questions, and cherished a choice collection of chaotic and contradictory convictions, which did not begin to clear until I reached the age of eighteen, when a lucky combination of influences transformed me into the anarchist that I have remained until this day. In the meantime, I had been an atheist, a materialist, an evolutionist, a prohibitionist, a free trader, a champion of the legal eight-hour day, a woman suffragist, an enemy of marriage, and a believer in sexual freedom.[4]

The major part of this "combination of influences" of which he wrote was a woman almost twice his age with whom Tucker fell passionately in love. The year was 1872, when Benjamin, barely eighteen, was in his second year at M.I.T. Already during his time in Boston, he had become interested in politics and was working in the presidential campaign of Horace Greeley. In this work, he became interested in the New England Labor Reform League and met Warren, Spooner, Greene, and Heywood. These strong voices of individualist anarchism soon converted him. The boy's interest in engineering faded quickly. He wanted nothing more than to be involved in the anarchist movement.

In February of 1873, the Labor Reform League became involved in a free-speech issue. Victoria Woodhull, the "terrible siren," anarchist, clairvoyant, ardent suffragist, and speaker in favor of free love could find no place to speak in Boston on the topic "Principles of Social Freedom." Young Benjamin took an active part in trying to see that Mrs. Woodhull was granted her right to be heard. Victoria had only recently been involved in a scandal that shocked most of New England, and the good people

VICTORIA WOODHULL

Photograph by
Matthew Brady

*Courtesy of The New-York
Historical Society, New York City*

of Boston simply would not tolerate her public appearance in their city. After a great deal of effort on Tucker's part it was arranged that she address the Convention of the New England Labor Reform League.

After her final speech to the group on February 25, Victoria hurried away, leaving her cloak behind in a rush to catch the night train to New York. Benjamin was sent after her. He arrived just as the train was about to pull away from the station, leaped on, and delivered the wrap to the lady, who shocked him by expressing her gratitude with a sudden and full kiss on the mouth.

Benjamin Tucker fell instantly in love, but he did not see Victoria again until the fall; instead of returning to M.I.T. he spent some months in New York, again devoting himself to finding places for Mrs. Woodhull to lecture. During this time he stayed with Victoria and her family until the summer of 1874, when they all left for Europe together. But two weeks later, Victoria and her sister returned to the United States while Benjamin stayed on until the beginning of 1875, when he returned to America more mature and an enthusiastic and eager anarchist.

For more than a year he worked with Ezra Heywood as associate editor of the latter's magazine, the *Word*. During that time, Tucker, like Thoreau, spent a short time in prison for refusing to pay taxes.

In 1877, Tucker decided it was time for him to initiate his own efforts for anarchism. Still somewhat timid and shy, he nonetheless was convinced enough about his social and economic views to make a convincing writer and speaker on them, and he founded his own periodical, the *Radical Review,* which lasted only four issues before its funds were exhausted.

So skillful a journalist was Tucker that the Boston *Daily Globe*, although aware that he was an anarchist, hired him as a reporter. Tucker stayed with the *Globe* for eleven years and was highly regarded both by the staff and the readers, even in a time when anarchists—especially after the Haymarket affair—were notably suspect; in all that time Tucker refused to write any story that he felt might compromise his anarchist principles.

After only a short time on the *Globe* he began to save money and to solicit donations, and on August 6, 1881, Tucker was able to start another periodical, *Liberty*, which, lasting until 1907, was the longest-lived of any radical American paper. In the first issue he wrote, "Monopoly and privilege must be destroyed, opportunity afforded, and competition encouraged. This is *Liberty's* work, and 'Down with Authority' her war-cry." Almost always, his style in *Liberty* was rational, incisive, and devastating when he criticized capitalist institutions.

In 1892, Tucker and *Liberty* moved to New York, where he worked on *Engineering Magazine*. He also set up a printing office and storeroom from which he issued low-priced editions of the best libertarian thinkers—Tolstoy, Shaw, Zola, and Wilde among them. Tucker's brand of anarchism was considered to be so rational and respectable that in 1899 he was invited to present the anarchist view of business combinations to the Chicago Conference on Trusts. One economist who heard his speech called it "the most brilliant bit of pure logic" delivered at the whole convention.[5]

To Tucker, the economic problems of American society were the most pressing. In an early issue of *Liberty* he wrote, "The whole loaf rightfully belongs to those who raise the wheat from the soil, grind it into flour, and bake it into bread, and not the smallest taste of it to the sharpers who deceive the unthinking masses into granting them a monopoly of the opportunities of performing these industrial operations, which opportunities they in turn rent back to the people on condition of receiving the other half of the loaf."[6]

The two most significant influences on this thought were Max Stirner and Herbert Spencer. Like Stirner, Tucker denied moral responsibility or the existence of any inherent rights and duties. The supreme law for men was self-interest, and from this Tucker developed the law of equal liberty: "Equal liberty means the largest amount of liberty compatible with equality and mutuality of respect, on the part of individuals living in society, for their respective spheres of action."[7] Each man would be equally free to assert his self-interest, and power would be the only measure of how far that assertion might go. " 'Mind your own business' is the only law of the anarchistic scheme."[8]

From equal liberty Tucker derived the freedom to resist invasion of that liberty. And the State represented "the embodiment of the principle of invasion." Again, "The anarchist defines government as invasion, nothing more or less. Protection against invasion, then, is the opposite of government. Anarchists, in favoring the abolition of government, favor the abolition of invasion, not protection against invasion."[9] Still, Tucker never wavered from his stand that it was wrong to attempt the overthrow of a government by force. Another form of State would only follow the revolution because men would still believe in the State. The anarchist's role was not to contribute violence, but to educate the public to an awareness that a State was not only unnecessary, it was evil.

Tucker thought it necessary to show the public and other anarchists the essential contradiction between what he called the two branches of socialism, libertarianism and anarchism on the one hand and state socialism on the other. In other words: Liberty *vs.* Authority. Both of these movements, he pointed out, derive their economics from the principle that labor is the true measure of price and then separately describe society as it should be. The great socialists—Warren, Proudhon, and Marx agreed that the only just wage of labor is its product; any other source of income is a way of depriving men of their just wages. The most usual forms of this deprivation—interest, rent, and profit—are merely kinds of usury and totally fraudulent. "The only reason the banker, the stockholder, the landlord, the manufacturer, and the merchant are able to exact usury from labor lies in the fact that they are backed by legal privilege, or monopoly; and . . . the only way to secure to labor the enjoyment of its entire product is to strike down monopoly."[10]

It is in how to destroy monopoly that state socialism and anarchism disagree. The first claims that "all the affairs of men should be managed by the government, regardless of individual choice," while the second is "the doctrine that all the affairs of men should be managed by individuals or voluntary associations, and that the State should be abolished." For the anarchist, free competition— the extreme definition of laissez-faire capitalism—is the universal rule. This simple distinction defines the essential unreconcilability of the two positions. The state socialist is as far from libertarian principles as the most headstrong fascist or open-minded democrat. Admit the State as arbiter of men's lives and you deny anarchism.

Even attempts to suppress vice are themselves crimes; the drunkard, the gambler, all social deviants have the right to pursue their lives as they choose until they choose to change.

Tucker was not successful in expanding the numbers of individualist anarchism. From the beginning of the 1900's he was talking to an increasingly diminished audience. Anarchists were joining the ranks of anarcho-communism led by Emma Goldman and Alexander Berkman, or becoming state socialists or communists, or leaving the radical movement entirely. The more direct approaches to immediate social action seemed to be the only reply to the multiplication of power that the capitalists and industrialists were enjoying. The extreme individualist could either join society, accepting some form of the State as inevitable, or retreat from it.

In 1907 "Benj. R. Tucker's Unique Book Shop" was opened in New York at 502 Sixth Avenue. It had the most impressive stock of libertarian literature in the world, and among the books were many translations and original volumes by Tucker himself. Over on Fourth Avenue, the office and printing plant were set up along with a large storeroom for extra book stock. On January 19, 1908, a fire swept through the whole building. The stock of paper and printing equipment was highly inflammable, and before the fire department could get the blaze under control the whole place was destroyed: all of Tucker's book stock, his printing equipment, his office records, and several important manuscripts of which there were no other copies. He did not even carry insurance. Although some friends tried to raise funds to cover the losses, they were not completely successful.

Even if the damages could have been repaired, it is doubtful whether Tucker would have gone back to his previous life. He was more than fifty years old and had fought in the libertarian movement his whole adult life. The fire just hurried a decision he'd been contemplating for some time. He gave up all political activity and moved with his family to France, where he lived until the start of World War I. At that time he moved once again —to England. Faced with the fact that some wars may be wrong but just, Tucker had a painful decision to make. It was even more difficult because many libertarian sympathizers saw the war less as one of ideals than as a battle between rival imperialists and industrial empires—a way, for example, for the munitions manufacturers to make more money.

Tucker abandoned his pacifist stand, however, and stated that the war had been caused by Prussian arrogance. In a 1914 letter to Joseph Labadie, one of his followers, he wrote:

> I favor the Allies because I pity the Belgian people, because I admire the British influences that make for liberty, because I feel some (though I regret to say a declining) concern for the American people, because I have a considerable sympathy for the *people* of Russia, and because I hate and fear the German people as a nation of domineering brutes bent on turning the whole world into a police-ridden paradise of the Prussian pattern.[11]

This is almost a total abandonment of principles he had developed over a lifetime. Tucker never again tried to have a voice in the anarchist movement. He no longer even wrote, confining his intellectual activities to clipping interesting articles from the newspapers and magazines he read. In a state of lethargy, Tucker moved to Monaco after World War I and lived there for twenty years, becoming more and more pessimistic as he saw the rise of one authoritarian State after another—the Russian Revolution and the birth of the communist State; the rise of Mussolini in Italy and Franco in Spain, and finally the birth of Nazism in Germany. As the world was on the brink of World War II, in 1939, Benjamin Tucker died at the age of eighty-five.

With Tucker's departure to Europe, American individualist anarchism soon faded into obscurity. He did have a few successors but they were never major figures. The most notable of them were John Beverly Robinson and Charles Leigh James.

Robinson, too, affirmed Stirner's egoism and focused his attention on "privilege," which was the ability of nonproducers to take a certain part of the product of a worker away from him (Tucker's half a loaf of bread). James had been a frequent contributor to *Liberty*. He chose to live with his family as a scholarly recluse, spending his time on a "Vindication of Anarchism," that was to trace its historical origins and give anarchy a philosophical basis.

Others included Labadie, the first Detroit organizer of the Knights of Labor and the possessor of an extraordinary library of libertarian literature now at the University of Michigan, and Victor S. Yarros, an individualist who focused his interest on the works of Spencer. Born in the Ukraine, Yarros came to the United States and at first spent his time with the collectivist immigrant anarchists in the East. In the early 1880's, however, he got to know some of the individualists and was slowly swayed to their point of view at a time when most of the conversion was in the opposite direction.

Eventually, there were only a handful of individualist anarchists left. The last of their spokesmen, Charles Erskine Scott Wood, was almost alone when he wrote in the early 1930's. At that time the United States was in the midst of a severe depression, and even the heads of big business, always against any restrictive legislation, were agreed that the government must step in and set up a system of controls to support and revitalize the economy. Yet in 1931, the year before Roosevelt was elected to the presidency, Wood published *Too Much Government*, a faint lament on the extent to which modern society had yielded to authority. Unable to believe seriously that it would be possible to combat the direction in which society was obviously tending, Wood still regretted that "We are interfered with and accustomed to control and direction from the cradle to the grave in thought, speech and act, in work and play, in morals and manners, in habits and costumes."[12]

12

The Red Scare

The American public responded to the threat of mad foreign anarchists with lit bombs in their hands with an hysterical hatred and fear. By the time the Haymarket affair was over the word "radical" was synonymous with "communist," "anarchist," and "dynamite." The news from Europe did nothing to ease the panic.

In 1893, three years before the Haymarket bomb, an anarchist named Vaillant exploded a bomb in the French Chamber of Deputies. When the judge accused him of endangering the lives of a number of innocent persons, Vaillant replied: "There can be no innocent bourgeois." The next year saw the explosions in a Paris café and a Barcelona theater, as well as the assassination of the President of the French Republic. Even though Congress had passed a law in 1894 prohibiting the admission of foreign anarchists, the Haymarket riot indicated that they might have been too late to save American democracy.

Two of the most feared of the alien anarchists were Emma Goldman (1869–1940), or "Red Emma," as the newspapers called her, and Alexander Berkman (1870–1936). Both had been born in Russia. Emma arrived in the United States at the age of seventeen with her sister Helena. Emma immediately went to work in a sweatshop in Rochester, sewing on overcoats for ten and a half hours a day under unhealthy conditions. The girls were not allowed to talk to one another or to sing while working. Even to leave one's place required permission from the foreman. For a work week of sixty-three hours she was paid $2.50.

Her family was staid and religious. They wanted Emma to settle down. Under their influence she married Jacob Kersner,

EMMA GOLDMAN

also an immigrant, but the marriage was not a happy one. Emma felt unrest and a growing concern with the problems of labor and of society as a whole. In 1889, just after her twentieth birthday, she left Kersner and arrived in New York on the hot, humid morning of August 15 with five dollars, a sewing machine, and her purse. She immediately checked her sewing machine and then went to visit an aunt and uncle, who were not happy with the unexpected visitor.

New York turned out not to be quite as she had imagined it. Emma had no money, no lodgings, and the sweltering August heat was almost unbearable. But she had heard of a café called Sachs, on Suffolk Street in Manhattan's Lower East Side. It was here that all the radicals met.

So Emma Goldman went to Sachs for dinner that night. While she was eating she heard a man call out, "Extra-large steak! Extra cup of coffee!" As she later wrote, she wondered to herself, "Who is that glutton?"[1] And turned to examine him.

"He was no more than a boy, hardly eighteen, but with the neck and chest of a giant. His jaw was strong and made more pronounced by his thick lips. His face was almost severe, but for his high, studious forehead and intelligent eyes." It was Alexander Berkman.

He in turn saw an intense, somewhat stocky, determined-looking young woman whose red cheeks and fiery eyes attracted him. The two introduced themselves, and he invited Emma to attend a lecture being given that night by Johann Most. On the way there she tripped and would have fallen, but Berkman held her arm. "I have saved your life," he said, and she answered, "I hope I may be able to save yours some day."

In this innocent evening began the lifelong friendship between the two and a working relationship for the cause of anarcho-communism that was for the readers of American newspapers, among the most notorious episodes of the 1890's.

ALEXANDER BERKMAN

Both Berkman and Emma Goldman had been affected by the Haymarket riot and were convinced that the hanging of four of the defendants was an appalling miscarriage of justice. When torture was used on the anarchists involved in the Barcelona explosion, and when a strike of steel workers in Homestead, Pennsylvania, was the scene of a number of vicious reprisals against the workers, Berkman concluded that it was time for an *attentat,* an attempted assassination to be considered "propaganda by deed."

Berkman determined that the deed having the most weight would be the assassination of one of the leading American capitalists, the man who was the chief opponent of labor in the Homestead steel strike, Henry Clay Frick. The resulting events were almost comic in their confusion.

First, for a week, Berkman experimented at night while Emma Goldman kept watch. He was trying to make a bomb, going by the directions given by Most in his *Science of Revolutionary Warfare*. But the device never worked.

They changed their plans. With only fifteen dollars left, Berkman went immediately to Pittsburgh while Emma tried to raise money for a new suit, so that he would look respectable when trying to get into Frick's office, and a gun. Emma was at a loss. She didn't know how to get money quickly. Romantic as always, she decided that if Sonia, Raskolnikov's girl friend in Dostoevski's *Crime and Punishment* could sell herself to men for her beloved, Emma Goldman could do the same.

She got a pair of high-heeled shoes and fancy clothes and tried to pick up some men. But she was unsuccessful. If one did happen to approach her, she turned him down. Finally, an old man bought her a beer and gave her ten dollars. But Emma owed five dollars on the clothes. In desperation, she wired her sister for fifteen dollars, saying she was sick.

Berkman, now in possession of a gun, turned up at Frick's office on Saturday, July 23, 1892. Without much trouble he managed to get in to see Frick, pulled out the gun, and fired, then fired again. As men poured into the room, Berkman took out a knife and wounded Frick twice with it. But none of the wounds was serious; Frick was laid up only a short time. Berkman was arrested on the spot.

Benjamin Tucker again found it necessary to dissociate himself and the other individualists from the deed. He wrote, "The worst enemy of the world is folly, and men like Berkman are its incarnation. It would be comparatively easy to dispose of the Fricks were it not for the Berkmans. . . . No pity for Frick, no praises for Berkman."[2]

At the trial, however, there was little room for an exposition of libertarian doctrine, and Berkman's only success seems to have been to encourage those who feared anarchists. He was, of course, convicted and sentenced to twenty-two years in prison, of which he served fourteen.

While the repudiation by Tucker, the individualists, and the bourgeois press did not surprise Emma or Berkman, that Johann

An 1892 woodcut depicting Berkman's attempted assassination of Henry Clay Frick

The Bettmann Archive

Most would turn his back on them was shocking. Most, only just out of prison, spoke on the subject and said that Berkman's act might well have been that of a crank or perhaps someone hired by Frick himself. He also said that he had overstressed the value of terrorism. Miss Goldman was furious. She appeared at his next lecture and ordered him to prove his statements. When he would not, she drew out a horsewhip and lashed him with it.

Emma went ahead with her defense of Berkman's deed and urged workers to use violence to attain their goals. In 1893 she delivered a speech in which she said, "Ask for work; if they do not give you work, ask for bread; if they do not give you work or bread, then take the bread."[3] For these words she was arrested, tried, and sentenced to one year in prison on Blackwell's Island in New York. On her release Emma Goldman went right back to agitation, speaking on workers' rights, Ibsen and modern drama, female suffrage, birth control, and most other aspects of the libertarian movement.

During the Spanish-American and Boer wars she delivered talks of a pacifist nature advocating that no one fight or in any way contribute to the wars. Oddly enough, she was not arrested for these speeches.

As the 1890's went on, "Red Emma" was sometimes used as a bogey by mothers to terrify their children into being good. She was the symbol of the evil and fanaticism of the radical movement. Yet in person her manner was inoffensive, even stolid and shy. If one did not know her name, she could have passed for a middle-aged housewife.

The anarchist menace seemed to strike once again. On September 6, 1901, at about four in the afternoon, the President of the United States, William McKinley, was in the midst of a tour of the Pan American Exposition in Buffalo, New York. During a reception at the Temple of Music, a medium-sized young man dressed in black moved up, as if to shake hands with the President. He had shy, childlike eyes and perhaps was not completely aware of his environment. The young man's hand was wrapped in a handkerchief, as if it were bandaged. He smiled as he came within two feet of McKinley, bowed, and extended his hand. Two

Czolgosz's assassination of President McKinley

shots rang out in the hall. McKinley stepped back a pace or two and then fell to the ground. He died eight days later.

The assassin, the shy young man, was Leon Czolgosz, an American of Polish descent, who during questioning declared he was an anarchist. Further investigation seemed to show that he had been inspired to the act, which Czolgosz believed was for the good of humanity, by a speech of Emma Goldman's. She was arrested in Chicago and kept in jail for a few weeks, until it became quite clear that no connection between the two could be proved.

In fact, Czolgosz was a solitary neurotic who attended few libertarian meetings of any kind. He had been denounced as a spy by one anarchist periodical, *Free Society*, and his only contact with Emma had been in July of 1901. On the twelfth of that month, while seeing her off on a train, a friend had said, "There is a fellow from Cleveland here who asks very peculiar questions.

If we do not wish to be bored by him, we must make our escape."[4]

Czolgosz was a self-avowed anarchist. But he had committed the act alone: "I had no accomplices. I did it for the dear people and I am ready to die."[5]

To President Theodore Roosevelt, Czolgosz was a typical anarchist, and his speech in Congress on the subject was a denunciation of all antistatists. In 1903, the United States Congress passed an even stiffer law excluding anarchists and other political refugees from America. It was supplemented in 1906 by the New York State criminal anarchy law.

The libertarian movement as a whole suffered greatly from the general fear of the public in these years. The anarchists declined greatly in number, and the exclusion of Europeans of this persuasion limited the group even more. Even Emma Goldman had serious doubts about her beliefs after McKinley's assassination and lived for some time in seclusion under the name of Miss E. G. Smith.

The doubts were only temporary, and she was soon back in the movement. With headquarters in New York, in 1906, Miss Goldman founded the periodical *Mother Earth*, which continued publication until 1917. Scheduled lectures were often canceled by hall owners or broken up by the police arbitrarily, whether the subject was birth control or anarchism. In Chicago, in 1908, for example, Chief of Police Shippy had issued orders that she was not to speak, but it became known that his ban was being ignored and that Emma was scheduled on the list of speakers at a meeting of the Literary Society of Women's Hall. During the evening, as soon as the clarinet solo she was to follow was over, the hundred or so police in the hall began to check their guns and get their clubs ready.

Emma Goldman got up to speak. Her first words were, "Ladies and gentlemen, I hope you will all remain quiet, no matter what happens."[6] She said nothing more. Captain Mahoney, the head of the police squad, immediately walked up to the platform and dragged her down from it, cursing her as he did so. When she asked to have her coat, he instructed one of the men, "Get the rags of this thing."

Again, in San Francisco, a soldier by the name of William Buwalder, who had been awarded a medal for bravery in action in the Philippines, attended several of Emma's speeches and after one of them shook hands with her. He was reported to the army authorities, court-martialed, and sentenced to five years at hard labor.[7]

It is true that Emma Goldman, along with the other anarchists, frequently used abusive and insulting language when they spoke of police, or of other representatives of authority, but antagonisms and the possibility of violence only grew when the police, who usually felt they were acting in a city's best interest, allowed their hostility to affect their actions.

While some anarchists were agitating from outside the labor movement itself for the birth of a nonauthoritarian society, anarcho-syndicalists were working effectively within the forces of labor. They were most powerful in the International Workers of the World (I.W.W.), the "Wobblies." This extremely radical labor union was founded in 1905 under the leadership of "Big Bill" Haywood. From the start the public identified the group with terrorism and destruction. And indeed the Wobblies were guilty of a certain amount of lawlessness and violence. The union did advocate social revolution and sabotage during strikes.

In 1908 the I.W.W. split. Chicago was the center of the old union, under the leadership of Haywood and Vincent St. John. This wing advocated direct action and was anarchistic in its philosophy. The other group, centered in Detroit, took the name of the Workers' International Union. With weakened effect the two groups continued to function until World War I, when—as organizations opposed to the American commitment in that war —they were suppressed, and under the Espionage Act Haywood was sentenced to twenty years in prison.

The anarcho-communists, too, were fascinated by the prospects of testing their beliefs by establishing model communities. One of the most interesting of these is the Home Colony, founded on Joe's Bay, an arm of Puget Sound, Washington, and incorporated under the laws of that state as the "Mutual Home Association." The location, only forty miles from Seattle, was arrived at during a time just following the failure of a socialist colony named Glennis in 1896. Disillusioned members of Glennis, George Allen, O. A. Verity, and F. F. Odell, built a boat and set out to explore Puget Sound in order to find a new home.

Joe's Bay was truly ideal, twenty-six acres of tall Douglas fir growing in a wilderness on the ocean, where ducks, clams, and game would furnish an abundant source of food. The men paid $2.50 an acre for their land, getting the deed with $5.00 down and a note for the rest. To earn the money Allen taught school and the others did odd jobs until the cash was gathered. Then in the spring of 1897 the three families settled on the land and established themselves as a mutualist, anarchist community. Each member paid the association for the land he or she occupied, but no one was allowed more than two acres, nor did anyone have title to the land, which was owned by the asociation.

The colonists built Liberty Hall, where Allen taught and where Emma Goldman came to lecture in 1899. After six months, six more families had come. The editor of the anarchist paper *Free Society* settled at Home Colony and began to issue a new paper.

Apparently the colonists were friendly and peaceable. However, in a Congressional hearing in 1919, the Home Colonists were called "argumentative," and it was asserted that there had been a public celebration there when McKinley was assassinated.

By 1900 there were about a hundred living on the land with thirty pupils in the school at Liberty Hall, where they read Mill, Huxley, Darwin, Warren, and Thoreau. At lectures the boys and girls learned that the only acceptable laws were natural ones. The peak membership is said to have been about five hundred, with two hundred and fifty to three hundred at the time of the 1919 hearings.

Whatever else might be said for or against the Home Colonists, they certainly were tenacious. When a journalist visited the site in the 1940's he found that the Colony still existed, or rather, one man, Jay Fox, whom the writer called "the sole surviving anarchist in the United States," still lived on the land and farmed it; he was a believer in the anarchist sentiments of the founders, as well.[8]

Among the nations sending large numbers of emigrants to the United States during the 1890's and in the early years of this century was Italy. There was a particularly large community near Paterson, New Jersey, because of the silk-weaving industry located there. This business afforded jobs similar to those the men and women had had in Lombardy and Piedmont in their native country.

A number of the residents of the Italian community in Paterson were anarcho-communists and syndicalists, and Paterson became the center of Italian-American antistatist activity. It was visited frequently by Enrico Malatesta, one of the most noted Italian anarchists. In New York City, Malatesta was a familiar figure on Bleecker Street and often had coffee in a little café on MacDougal Street, where his dignified bearing and the perennial wide-brimmed slouch hat marked him out to passers-by. In the winter of 1899, Malatesta delivered a series of lectures on anarchism that were attended by many of his immigrant countrymen.

One of the most notable of these was Gaetano Bresci, who had come to the United States in 1895 from his home near Florence. He was delicate-looking, and often talked of his fear of consumption. Even at the age of thirty-five, he was already old-looking, stooped, with a thin, sallow face. Bresci went home to Paterson and organized a group of anarchists as "L'Era Nuova" (The New Era). Verbal expression was not enough for Bresci, however. In 1900 he bought a gun and began to talk about his health again, saying that for his own good he thought he should spend a few months back in Italy with his mother. While preparations for the trip were being made, he practiced with the revolver in the woods near Weehawken while his wife and daughter gathered wild flowers. Bresci sailed in May. He had a simple plan; the only tool was a cheap American gun. There were no confederates, no meetings to arrange, no complicated schemes to synchronize: Bresci sought out King Humbert of Italy in the city of Manza and when he found him, killed him.

Even with Bresci gone, under the leadership of Luigi Galliani and Fermino Gallo, the group continued to be active. Many years later, a number of their sons formed the Francisco Ferrer Association, naming it after a Spanish anarchist who had been killed. Most of this anarchist association's members were under the age of twenty-one, and the group began just as World War I spread to the United States. The boys were all pacifists; most refused to serve in the army during the war, and strong antidraft propaganda was circulated by them. After the war, the Ferrer Association set up a community of about twenty families in Stelton, New Jersey, where in the summer the population rose to about two hundred. This group's most notable achievement was in education. They had a very modern school in New York City that, despite the antigovernment schooling given the students, was noted for its innovations in teaching methods.

The boys in the Ferrer Association were not the only anarchists to circulate antiwar and antidraft materials and to be arrested for it. Emma Goldman and Alexander Berkman, now out of prison, were prominent in organizing pacifist demonstrations and in speaking against the war. They founded a No-Conscription League that agitated against the legality and morality of the draft. Appeals were made to workers to refuse to load ammunition, and men were told to refuse to be coerced into military service.

One of the pieces of propaganda was headed, "Refuse to Kill or be Killed." Its text read:

You are against murder and bloodshed, you have no special grievances against the working class of Germany. All you ask for is to get along peacefully, express yourself, make a living, and take care of your family. You don't want war and you didn't ask the president or anyone else to declare war. . . .

No man is brave or strong or lucky enough to escape killing when once he has the uniform on. . . . Don't try to bluff yourself or anyone else. You must realize that if you join the army you will do just as you are told to do. . . .

If you think murder is wrong, REFUSE TO JOIN THE ARMY or any military body. Then if the government wants to kill you or put you in jail, you will have done your part and have been faithful to your conscience and humanity and the world will be the better for your courage and determination.[9]

The anarchists refused to recognize this was as being one of ideals, and they did all they could to arouse the disaffiliated or neutral against it. Not only did it seem to them to have been invented by the capitalists for their own profit, but it was also immoral to conceive of the workers of one nation fighting their natural allies, the workers of another. Their speeches were given wide publicity in the daily press. The newspapers held their agitation up to the readers as a dangerous example of foreign espionage in the country, playing on the fact that most of the anarchists were foreign-born themselves, or the children of immigrants. From 1917 on, men and women with German-sounding names were suspect, no matter what their true sentiments were. These daily exposures of German and communist plots were almost all based on flimsy or nonexistent evidence.

But naturally enough the patriots in America felt that this war, which was going to be the "war to end all wars" required the dedication and faith of all Americans. The anarchists' pacifism to them seemed actually to be treason and a threat to democracy.

A pacifist demonstration at the Capitol, May 13, 1917

Culver Pictures In

On July 15, 1917, Emma Goldman, Alexander Berkman, and several of their colleagues were arrested and indicted for violation of the new Espionage Act. Emma and Berkman were convicted—after trying to use the trial as a platform for their views on pacifism, the war, and anarchism—and each was sentenced to two years in prison, fined $10,000, and faced probable deportation on release from jail. These were extremely light sentences compared to those given other pacifists at the time.

Before going to prison they issued a joint declaration:

Be of good cheer, good friends and comrades. We are going to prison with light hearts. To us it is more satisfactory to stay behind bars than to remain MUZZLED in freedom. Our spirit will not be daunted, nor our will broken. . . .

The light of liberty burns low just now. But do not despair, friends. Keep the spark alive. The night cannot last forever.[10]

But the night grew increasingly darker.

The success of the Russian Revolution only increased the fear throughout the world. No country seemed to be safe from the "Red Menace."

As soon as World War I was over, economic conditions in America contributed to a general feeling of unrest. More than four million workers were employed in industries devoted to manufacturing war goods. In 1919 they had not yet been converted to peaceful manufactures and many were out of work. Also, a postwar inflation gripped the country and the cost of living rose alarmingly, in 1919 becoming ninety-nine per cent higher than it had been in 1913.[11] There naturally was a certain amount of tension between management and workers. Only this time, the sympathy of the public, which before the war had reached some understanding of labor's position, was wholeheartedly with the industrialists. There were about 3,600 strikes in 1919, and almost all of them were unsuccessful.

To further unsettle the country, President Wilson, who had been a vigorous leader during the war, suffered a nervous breakdown, followed by a severe stroke, from which he never fully recovered. For the rest of his term of office, until 1921, he was not fully involved in the country's government and the heads of various departments, sometimes in consultation with Mrs. Wilson, took an unusual amount of independent authority.

America still had not recovered from the surge of superpatriotism brought on by the war. Those libertarians, radicals, or members of religious sects who had been pacifists during the war had shown their colors; they were still spies and servants of masters other than the United States after the Armistice was signed. The Espionage Act of 1917 had been followed by the Sedition Act of 1918, which made it unlawful to "utter, print, write, or publish any disloyal, profane, scurrilous, or abusive language about the form of government of the United States, or the Constitution of the United States, or the uniform of the Army or Navy of the United States."[12]

In all sincerity many public officials and a substantial proportion of the citizenry believed that America was being threatened by an enemy that was numerous and powerful enough to warrant strong countermeasures in defense of democracy.

In a Congressional hearing late in 1920, the testimony included a long quotation from a speech by Judge George W. Anderson, who had been attorney general in Boston from November 1914 to October 1917. In his address to the Harvard Liberal Club in January of that year, the judge had said:

> What I now say I say entirely on my own responsibility, but I say it after exchanging views with many others having analogous responsibilities during the war period. If in fact the pro-German plots were no adequate basis for public fear, and for legislature and official activities against the right of the individual and social liberty, it is quite possible that the "red menace" promoted in large part by the same notoriety-seeking individuals and newspapers, ought not to frighten us to death.
>
> Now, I assert on my best judgment, grounded on the information that I can get that more than 90 per cent of the advertised and reported pro-German plots never existed. . . . I doubt the red menace having more basis in fact than the pro-German peril. I assert the significant fact that many of the same persons and newspapers that were faking pro-German plots are now promoting "the red terror." [13]

During these same hearings, thirty-five years before the Mc-

Carthy hearings of the 1950's, one of the witnesses referred to those who incited the public to fear of the "red menace" as "witch hunters." Looking back on this period, it is apparent that some men enlarged a real problem and advanced the idea of a threat from the communists and anarchists not to protect the United States so much as to aid political careers, capture readers for newspapers, or gain such intimidation of labor that wages and hours would no longer be liberalized. Because so much of the anti-red propaganda was a hoax, the truth of some of the claims of communist infiltration was lost.

One last terrible episode occurred before national hysteria had reached its peak. On April 28, 1919, it was discovered that a bomb had been sent through the mail to Mayor Ole Hanson of Seattle, one of the strongest opponents of radicalism in America. No one was injured, but the next day another bomb was delivered to a former senator from Georgia, Thomas W. Hardwick, and this time the family's maid opened the package. In the ensuing explosion she lost both hands and Mrs. Hardwick was severely burned on the face. In all, thirty-six bombs were found, although none of the others detonated, and no one else was hurt. It was the intent of a group or of an individual to hurt or kill a number of notable conservatives. While again the mysterious bombers were not found, it seemed that this time "reds" had been trying to destroy property and persons.

The Chicago *Tribune* assisted the growing panic by printing "BEWARE BOX IF IT COMES THROUGH MAIL—Do Not Open It— Call the police bomb squad." Mayor Hanson said, "I trust Washington will buck up and hang or incarcerate for life all the anarchists."[14]

This time there was concrete evidence that almost certainly had not been manufactured by fanatics or ambitious publicity seekers. While no evidence indicated that anarchists were definitely involved, it was a reasonable assumption that some radicals had done the deed.

The bomb scare was followed by the largest radical May Day parade up to that time in the United States. There were riots in New York, Boston, and Cleveland. Frequently, radical papers or organization headquarters were broken into by members of the armed forces or civilians and destroyed.

The hysteria was never given a chance to die down. On the evening of June 2, bombs exploded anew, and this time two persons were killed. The homes of law-enforcement officials, a mayor, a Philadelphia jeweler, and a Paterson silk manufacturer were bombed. The most publicized of the attacks was on the home of the Attorney General of the United States, A. Mitchell Palmer. Just after the Palmer family went to bed, the entire front of his house was destroyed, and apparently the bomb thrower with it. Along with the remains of the man were found several copies of a circular headed "Plain Words":

We are not many, perhaps more than you dream of though, but are determined to fight to the last, till [no] man remains buried in your bastilles, till [no] hostage of your working classes is left to the tortures of your police system, and will never rest till your fall is complete and the laboring masses have taken possession of all that rightfully belongs to them.

There will have to be bloodshed: we will not dodge; there will have to be murder: we will kill because it is necessary; there will have to be destruction: we will destroy to rid the world of your tyrannical institutions. [The statement was signed, "The Anarchist Fighters."][15]

From clothing and other evidence the bomb thrower was identified as an Italian alien from Philadelphia, but his name was never discovered. This evidence and the attack on the Paterson silk manufacturer seemed to point to the New Era anarchists and Galliani as being involved in the plot. It is very doubtful that the circular was a forgery, and some anarchist group was certainly involved in this series of bombs. Although no proof of Galliani's guilt could be established, he was deported.

The public now was thoroughly frightened, and investigations into the depth of the red menace began. The Justice Department received a special appropriation of half a million dollars to find and arrest anarchists. Oddly enough, not one bomb maker or thrower was found.

The most famous of the investigations was undertaken by the New York State Lusk Committee, whose sessions began on

June 12, 1919, in New York City Hall. At once the committee obtained a number of search warrants and began to raid radical centers throughout the city. On August 14, for example, the Union of Russian Workers—an anarcho-syndicalist group located at 133 East 15th Street—was raided and searched, the warrant being executed by members of the police bomb squad.

The police found, in a decaying renovated private house, a schoolroom, used for the education of adults, equipped with a blackboard and crude desks and benches. Throughout the building large stocks of anarchist literature were seized and read into the committee records. Three Russian immigrants were charged with criminal anarchy and later deported.

In all the Lusk Committee succeeded in getting only about seventy-five indictments for criminal anarchy during the course of its hearings, yet that same year, before the House of Representatives, Charles D. Newton, attorney general of New York, testified that in his city there were between 300,000 and 500,000 men and women "organized with the idea of overthrowing the government by force or violence."[16] And, he said, most of these were aliens. The entire alien population of the city, including those born abroad or whose fathers had emigrated to America, was just under two million. In other words, Newton was saying that up to one-quarter of the European immigrants were communists and anarchists. The figures were preposterous, but they were believed by the public. Again, no one would claim that there were not some—perhaps five hundred or a thousand—persons in New York City who advocated the violent overthrow of the American government. And, if these persons meant what they said (which, as the case of Johann Most demonstrates, is doubtful) then they were a danger to the country. But to multiply their numbers a thousandfold and to find imaginary plots all over the place did the democratic system no service.

By fall of 1919, the "red menace" had taken possession of the United States. A crusading group of superpatriots made it their business to hunt out "radicals" wherever they might be and punish them. Since they never clearly defined what a radical or an anarchist was, they suspected anyone whose views were not theirs.

This greatly enlarged the list of potential suspects, so that it seemed that antigovernment forces did exist in large numbers. Among the organizations strangely supposed to be bolshevist were the American Civil Liberties Union, the League of Women Voters, and the Foreign Policy Association.

The Lusk Committee came up with some supposed evidence indicating that there was strong communist influence in Negro communities. They held up as evidence a number of ugly race riots in many cities, especially Chicago and Washington, D.C. The riots, of course, rather than being communist-inspired were the beginnings of a civil rights movement.

Other civil disturbances followed, and a tendency toward mob violence grew. One terrible incident occurred in Centralia, Washington, when three members of the American Legion, in a group that had been heckling some I.W.W. pacifists, were killed by Wobblies in the riot that ensued. One of the Wobblies, Wesley Everest, was beaten almost to death, taken in a car to the Chehelis River and emasculated en route. He was hanged from a bridge by a rope the Legionnaires declared was too short, hanged again, pulled back a second time, and when he was pushed over yet a third time and managed to cling to the bridge, the men near him trampled on his fingers until he let go. While he was hanging there, his body was riddled with bullets. When the body was returned to Centralia, the coroner, in a dreadfully cynical verdict, said that Everest "went to the Chehelis River bridge and committed suicide. He jumped off with a rope around his neck and then shot himself full of holes."[17]

The spirit of hatred was consuming the United States. If any one man was especially responsible for this, it was the Attorney General of the United States, A. Mitchell Palmer, who from November 1919 through January of 1920 conducted what is sometimes called "Palmer's reign of terror." Palmer, who had been raised in a religious Quaker household, was an intelligent and able lawyer. While it is true that he undertook his campaign against the "red menace" partly because of a demand by the public, it is also true that he saw a situation that could also be used to his own political advantage: a disabled President with a weak control on government could never closely oversee his department, and with his eye on the White House, Palmer tried to use the national hysteria to his own advantage.

With the half-million dollars that Congress had appropriated, Palmer set up in the Bureau of Investigation an efficient anti-radical division under the leadership of the young, eager J. Edgar Hoover. Under Hoover's skillful direction a card file was built up with information on the location and behavior of every known and suspected radical.

Palmer was then ready to move. On November 7, throughout the country, under Palmer's direction the Union of Russian Workers' headquarters in each city was raided and notable members were picked up at their homes. The police had little sympathy with this group of "traitors," and many of the arrested men were beaten and mishandled. And, while there was a criminal anarchy law to support the arrests, the use of search warrants and warrants for arrest was frequently ignored.

The next day in New York City, under the guidance of the

A. MITCHELL PALMER

Lusk Committee, 700 police raided 73 radical centers and 500 were arrested. In all, about 3,000 persons were held; most eventually were released, but those who were aliens and believed deportable were turned over to the proper authorities; 246 men and 3 women—including Emma Goldman and Alexander Berkman, taken from their jails—were interned on Ellis Island and deported from the United States on December 21, 1919, on the S.S. *Buford*, the "Soviet Ark." The ship arrived in Finland on January 17, 1920, and the group was conducted across the border into Russia on January 19.

Only a few of the deportees were notable anarchists and communists (and most were anarcho-communists); most had never been convicted of any acts of terrorism, nor had they been convicted of criminal anarchy, sedition, or any other crime. Seven were criminals or social misfits and 199 of the deportees had been picked up in raids on the Union of Russian Workers. They were only theoretical anarchists.

On January 2, 1920, it was the turn of the communists. In national raids more than 8,000 were arrested, of whom about 450 were finally held for deportation. With these raids died the image of the United States as a haven for political refugees.

Even the method of taking the *Buford* deportees into custody was unfortunate. As mentioned, many had been arrested without warrants. They were imprisoned without bail on Ellis Island, and while attorneys still hoped for their release, on the night of December 20, the 249 were brusquely informed by guards to get ready to board the ship. No relatives or friends were allowed to say a final good-bye. On board the ship there was a guard of 250 soldiers, about one for each prisoner. A sentry stood day and night before each cabin door. The deportees were allowed only one hour a day on deck. After a little time in Russia, the anarchists discovered that the bolshevik government was even more oppressive than that in America, and both Emma Goldman and Berkman wrote of their disillusionment.

Instead of focusing on a famous radical, let us look at the case of one of the obscure Russians on the *Buford*. His name was Paul Bosco. In 1911, at the age of twenty-seven, he had come to the United States from his home in southern Russia, near the German frontier. Bosco had been sentenced to ten years in prison—which immediately set him off from most of the others being deported. The sentence was for violating the Espionage Act and distributing a pacifist pamphlet "The Price We Pay" during World War I. Upon being questioned, Bosco asserted that he was not an anarchist. "I do not believe in the overthrow of law," he said, "but whenever laws are against the people I see no reason why the people should not resist their enforcement by force, if it is attempted to enforce the law by force. Whenever Congress passes a law that is contrary to the interests of the people and contrary to the rights guaranteed by the Constitution, then the people are justified in resisting the enforcement of such a law." Bosco repeatedly referred to rights granted by the Constitution, and said he did not object to anarchism *because* the Constitution did not forbid it. Even at his most defiant, saying that he hoped on his release from prison to see the red banner over the American flag, Bosco still added, "I don't call that anarchy because the red flag is an international emblem."

The committee said that although Bosco did not call his beliefs anarchistic, they were so by definition. But Bosco's appeal to the Constitution had a weight that the committee did not recognize. He said to his examiners at the end, "The Constitution of the United States gives every man in the United States a right to express his opinion. . . . I think the Constitution guarantees freedom for foreign people the same as for United States citizens, therefore I try to exercise my privilege."[18]

The red scare soon subsided, although a fear of radicals, particularly alien radicals, persisted in the United States at least until World War II. One is left uneasy by the whole event. The anarchists were not innocent; they did incite to violence, they did not become citizens of this country, they (in some numbers) had been responsible for many violent episodes resulting in deaths and injuries, and they did advocate the violent overthrow of the American government. Yet their opponents allowed prejudice to influence them and did not always observe the laws or the Constitution in their zeal.

13

The Shoemaker and the
Fish Peddler: Sacco and Vanzetti

If the Haymarket riot and its aftermath separated liberals and radicals into seemingly irreconcilable factions, another sensational trial and death sentence brought them together again. And this time, most of the intellectual community in the United States united with them. Just beginning to feel their power and identity as a separate class, the intellectuals were noticing a sense of alienation from the rest of American society. Most of them were liberals, and they were ready to find a cause to rally round. They found it in the "American Dreyfus case," the Sacco-Vanzetti trial. Eventually, many noted American writers and historians became partisans of Sacco and Vanzetti. Among them were John Dos Passos, Dorothy Parker, Heywood Broun, Edna St. Vincent Millay, Walter Lippman, Van Wyck Brooks, Samuel Eliot Morison, and Arthur M. Schlesinger.

For those who found the final verdict unjust, the parallels to the Dreyfus case were remarkable. Dreyfus had been a captain in the French army. He was never particularly popular with the extremely conservative army officers, who considered him a "foreigner" because he was a Jew. When it became evident that some member of the staff with which Dreyfus was associated had given French military information to other countries, Dreyfus was accused and tried. But the evidence at his trial had been fabricated by some officers in the army because they wanted to conceal the name of the real traitor. Without a fair trial or a proper opportunity to defend himself, Dreyfus was sentenced to life imprisonment on Devil's Island, a penal colony off the coast of French Guiana. His wife, and a few friends who believed in his innocence, tried to arouse the French people to protest the miscarriage of justice. For a number of years they were ignored. Then, slowly the intellectuals of France came to his defense, notably Emile Zola, in his pamphlet *I Accuse*. Years later, a reinvestigation proved Dreyfus innocent and he was pardoned.

The whole massive Sacco and Vanzetti affair began simply enough. Christmas Eve 1919 was a Wednesday, and working men were waiting for their pay envelopes before going home for the holiday evening. At the L. Q. White Shoe Company, in Bridgewater, Massachusetts, the paymaster, while carrying the $33,000 payroll, was attacked by three "foreign-looking" men. One, bareheaded with a dark mustache and a long black coat, carried a shotgun; the other two carried pistols. The bandits were unsuccessful; no one was hurt. During their investigation of the case, Pinkerton detectives were told by an informer that the criminals were anarchists.

This information could have been authentic. But this was at the very height of the "red scare," and it would have been tempting to try to throw the blame on a group that was already suspected of every sort of crime imaginable. At any rate, the robbers were not caught.

A rather ordinary police investigation ensued, and the case was filed away as unsolved. Nothing more would have been heard of it if it had not been for a much more violent crime, also committed by foreign-looking men, in the nearby town of South Braintree. This time it was spring, April 15, 1920, and several people in the small community had noticed some strangers in town.

At the Slater & Morrill office—again it was a shoe factory— the paymaster, Frederick Parmenter, was getting ready to take the payroll over to the main factory building. At three o'clock, he and his guard, Alessandro Berardelli, took the money in steel cash boxes downstairs and outside.

Parmenter, a genial brown-haired man in his mid-forties, short and heavily built, must have been glad of a short walk in the spring sunshine. The two men walked down Pearl Street and met Jimmy Bostock, a machine repairman, for whom Parmenter had a message. They moved on and passed two strangers. One of the men had a cap on and the other wore a dark hat.

As Berardelli came up to them, the two men lunged at him. The man with the cap grabbed hold of him and threatened him with a pistol. When the guard fought back, he was shot three times. Parmenter turned around and was himself shot by the same man, first in the chest and then, as he tried to get away, in the back.

In the meantime, the man in the dark hat gathered up the cash boxes. A dark car (first called a Hudson by the eyewitnesses and later a Buick) came up to meet the holdup men. Another bandit was standing on the running board, guarding the car with his gun. When they came opposite Berardelli, this man also fired at the guard. The two other men, with the money, leaped into the back seat. The third gunman fired at the factory a few times and then got into the front seat. The robbers managed to get away before anyone could even reach Parmenter or Berardelli. The guard, by the time help came, was already dead; Parmenter died of wounds in the hospital. The robbers were now double murderers.

Before the paymaster died, he managed to describe the men who had attacked him. One, he said, was short, dark-skinned, dark-haired, and heavy. The other was short and thin. The doctor performing Berardelli's autopsy removed the bullets and marked them on the bottom with needle scratches. It was his opinion that the man might have lived but for the last bullet, fired into him point-blank by the bandit standing outside the car. This bullet had three needle marks put on it by the doctor and was considered the fatal one.

The identity of the gang was a mystery. No one in particular was suspected, nor would they have been if it had not been for an odd coincidence. In West Bridgeport, close to the scene of both robberies, lived an Italian anarchist by the name of Ferruchio Coacci, also known as Ercole Parrecca. Coacci had recently been ordered deported. He had been told to report to the Immigration Service on April 16, the day after the robbery. On that day he called to ask for more time because his wife was ill. Suspecting that Coacci was just trying to get more time or avoid deportation completely, Inspector Root of the Immigration

Service asked Chief of Police Michael Stewart to go with him to Coacci's lodgings that night in order to check out the story. Stewart said he was going to be busy (he was appearing in an amateur play production) and that West Bridgewater was not in his jurisdiction, but he did agree to send a night patrolman with Root.

Coacci was living in the home of Mario Buda, who was known around town as Mike Boda. Boda, a dapper man with a short, well-trimmed mustache, was regarded as being of somewhat questionable character, and later on did become a bootlegger. Like Coacci, Boda was an anarchist.

When Root and the patrolman arrived at the house, they were given quite a different story. This time the deportee claimed that his wife was all right and that he was ready to leave at once. He had $200 and said he didn't have to leave any of it for his family because they had enough.

Chief Stewart, when he heard of this from the patrolman, began to think. He knew that the robbers in the December 24 holdup were supposed to have been anarchists, and that the April 15 gang had also been described as foreign-looking. It was possible that the same group had committed both crimes and that the anarchists Boda and Coacci were a part of the gang. His suspicions were given more weight the next day when, close to Boda's house, the stolen car that had been used in the robbery was found.

Pretending that a photograph of Coacci was needed by the Immigration Service, Stewart got into the house and began searching it. None of the payroll money was found. But the policeman produced a gun filled with three different kinds of bullets. The bullets used in the South Braintree robbery also had been of varied kinds. The gun was Boda's, but Coacci, too, had a gun, a Savage automatic. He, however, was not available for questioning; the ship taking him back to Italy had sailed.

Stewart was suspicious of Boda after the search and his questioning, and Boda was afraid. That same day, Mrs. Coacci and her children moved to another house in South Braintree; Boda stored his car in the garage of Simon Johnson and left quietly for Boston. He hid there for several weeks in the home of an Italian friend.

The sudden disappearance confirmed Stewart's suspicions. The police chief instructed Johnson to let him know as soon as he heard from Boda. It was a clever move. Only a few days later, on May 5, Boda, a man on a motorcycle, and two others who seemed to be his friends came back to South Bridgewater for the car. Mrs. Johnson went to a friend's to call the police and passed two of the men Boda had brought with him. One of them, wearing a felt hat, had a remarkable mustache—very long and drooping—for she noticed it at once. The other wore a derby hat, an overcoat, and was clean-shaven. Perhaps suspecting that Johnson had been in touch with the police, Boda and the cyclist, Ricardo Orciani, left together. The other two walked to the trolley-car stop nearby and boarded the next car to Brockton.

Shortly after the four left, Chief Stewart arrived at the garage. It was not possible to find Boda and Orciani, but he could get the others. Stewart called the Brockton police headquarters and told the police there that two foreigners on the next trolley had just tried to steal an automobile. As the trolley pulled into the town, police boarded it and arrested the two as "suspicious characters." The clean-shaven one put his hand under his overcoat and was ordered to stop and keep his hands "outside his clothes." When he did the same thing a second time, the policeman said, "Mister, if you put your hand in there again you are going to get into trouble."[1]

At police headquarters the two suspects were searched and questioned. The clean-shaven one's name was Nicola Sacco. He was a short, muscular, handsome young man in his late twenties, whose use of English was very limited. The officers found that he was carrying a fully loaded 32-caliber Colt automatic and, in addition, twenty-three cartridges of different sorts. Sacco also had a penciled draft in Italian announcing an anarchist meeting. In response to questions by Chief Stewart on the night of his arrest Sacco said that he knew neither Coacci nor Boda, that he was not an anarchist or a communist, and that he carried a gun because there were a lot of bad men around. Sacco was married, with a seven-year-old son, Dante, and his wife was pregnant. He had had a good job in the Three K Shoe Company, and as a skilled worker made as much as $60 to $70 a week.

Sacco's employer, Michael Kelley, liked him and gave him extra work so that he could make even more money. One of these additional jobs required tending the plant furnace after hours, and when Sacco went to do this he took his gun with him. He was known as a quiet, dependable worker who liked nothing better than to work in the garden during his free hours. He was an avowed atheist and refused to go into any church, but his wife Rosina was a devout Catholic. Sacco read on occasion, but then only anarchist tracts.

One of the questions raised by the prosecution was why this steady, well-paid worker had suddenly quit his job. Sacco was able to produce evidence that his mother was ill. He had left his job on May 1 because he and his family were planning to sail for Italy in a few days.

The man whose mustache Mrs. Johnson had found so memorable was also an Italian immigrant. His name was Bartolomeo Vanzetti. The police search revealed that he had been armed with a 38-caliber Harrington & Richardson pistol loaded with two kinds of shell, and four shotgun shells. Vanzetti was only a few years older than Sacco, thirty-two at the time of the arrest, but to many he seemed at least ten years older. Nor was he as handsome as Sacco. Vanzetti had not led as regular a life; he was unmarried and a fish peddler. His thin face and prominent cheekbones seemed only to increase the effect of his large, drooping mustache, and the children in the neighborhood where he lived called him "Bart the Beard." Vanzetti was more intelligent than his friend, and while he did not have much more familiarity with English, was extremely well read.

When he was questioned, he, too, denied knowing Boda and Coacci. Also, on being asked if he was an anarchist, Vanzetti replied that he was a little different and liked to think a little differently. Like Sacco, he had no permit for the gun he was carrying. His reason for having a weapon was that as a fish peddler working alone he needed it for protection.

VANZETTI and SACCO

It was immediately obvious that Sacco and Vanzetti were lying. They knew Boda well and had come with him to pick up his car. They were both anarchists, and for some time both had been active in Galliani's New Era group. The first serious question about their innocence arises here. If the two men were innocent, why did they lie?

The answer given at the trial was that while they were innocent of robbery and murder, they still had something to hide. Both men claimed that they thought they were being arrested as radicals. This is not at all unlikely considering the number of such arrests being made at the time. Vanzetti had just been in New York, and he had been warned there that more Justice Department raids were going to come soon. In fact, Sacco and Vanzetti had come with Boda for the car so that they could use it to pick up incriminating anarchist pamphlets being stored at the homes of sympathetic antistatists. The men would naturally in this case have been afraid of arrest and deportation and they would have wanted to protect Boda and Orciani by claiming not to know them. This, too, would explain the apparent "consciousness of guilt" that weighed so heavily against them.

But their reasons for being armed were less credible. Although they might have thought they needed protection, the excuse was a weak one, especially on Sacco's part.

After the first examination, which took about ten minutes for the two men, both were locked in jail cells to spend their first night behind bars. The police at the jail did nothing to make Sacco and Vanzetti less afraid. They were hostile and pretended to be getting ready to shoot them both.

The next day the motorcycle was traced to Ricardo Orciani. He was arrested, and the police found a revolver in his bureau drawer. On being asked why he had a weapon, Orciani said it just "happened" to be there. Unlike the other two under arrest, Orciani never showed fear of the police. He was calm and assured at all times and refused to answer any questions.

While Orciani was being apprehended, District Attorney Frederick Gunn Katzmann was questioning Sacco and Vanzetti. Katzmann had been born into a poor family and had spent his life forging a career for himself, working to put himself through Harvard and night law school in Boston. Now, as District Attorney of Norfolk and Plymouth counties, he had a flourishing career and could look forward to a judgeship at the least and perhaps to becoming attorney general of the state. In his late forties, plump, well-fed, and snappily dressed, Katzmann was a successful man. To him, the only drawback to his future seemed to be his foreign-sounding name, about which he was sensitive.[2]

When asked what he had been doing on April 15, Sacco replied that he'd been at work. Vanzetti wasn't sure, but then he thought he'd been selling fish. Katzmann had already checked at the Three-K factory and knew that Sacco had not been there on the 15th. He finished his first series of questions sure of Sacco's guilt but doubtful about Vanzetti. Later in the day a number of witnesses to the Bridgewater and South Braintree crimes were brought to see Sacco and Vanzetti. Here, too, procedure was not all it might have been. There was no line-up, and no other men were shown to the observers. The two suspects were put before the group by themselves and told to stand, kneel, act as if they were shooting, and put on and take off their hats. Most of the witnesses were unsure, but there were several who were absolutely positive on their identification of Vanzetti. One of these was questionable, because the man had already vividly described the bandit's mustache as being small and closely trimmed, changing his story only after he saw Vanzetti. A few more witnesses tentatively identified Sacco, not for the first robbery but for the murder at South Braintree.

But the state's case was not solid on this point. One person identified Vanzetti as the driver of the getaway car, but Vanzetti did not know how to drive. When shown Orciani after his arrest, three witnesses said that he had been at South Braintree and one that he had been at Bridgewater. Yet Orciani proved by his time card at work that he had been on his job both days. Still, there was always the chance that some friend punched his time card for him.

The evidence was sufficient for Katzmann, however. The district attorney prepared indictments of Sacco and Vanzetti for carrying concealed weapons, and Orciani was charged with speeding and with not having a tail light on his motorcycle. All three were held without bail.

Later, with additional eyewitness identification of Vanzetti for the earlier crime, it was decided that he be tried first for it, separately. In his defense, the man claimed that he had been selling eels in the nearby town of South Plymouth throughout the day of the Bridgewater robbery. He was so sure because it was

Christmas Eve, the day when all Italians buy eels for their holiday dinner. Moreover, he had been accompanied by young Beltrando Brini, only thirteen at the time, who testified for him.

The judge was Webster Thayer. He was sixty-three at the time of the first trial, of remarkably short stature, with a leathery, wrinkled face that made him seem even older. Judge Thayer presented a somber appearance as he sat in the courtroom, his narrow mouth drawn in, and his pince-nez gleaming in the light. Thayer had already heard one case involving anarchists. There, although he conducted a fair trial, he had shown himself to be a bitter foe of antistatism. But the defense lawyers at first did not concern themselves with this problem since Thayer was known for his fairness in the courtroom.

But an odd thing happened. Once Thayer learned that Sacco and Vanzetti were anarchists, he took a most improper action, writing a letter to John Aiken, the chief justice of Massachusetts, requesting that he be allowed to preside over the trial.

At the trial, Vanzetti presented the evidence that he had been selling eels. Young Brini testified, but he was too young to carry much weight in court, and District Attorney Katzmann hurt his testimony on cross-examination by complimenting the boy at one point for having done such a good job of memorizing his story.

Forty years after he testified, Brini was interviewed by the author Francis Russell. He still insisted that he had been with Vanzetti on December 24, 1919. In support of this is a receipt found by the defense several years after the trial for a barrel of eels received by Vanzetti on December 20.

But the defense again took a questionable position. Vanzetti failed to take the stand in his own defense, and this counted heavily against him, impressing the jurors with the probability of his guilt. Vanzetti later claimed that his lawyer, John Vahey, refused to let him testify. But Vahey said that he had insisted that Vanzetti take the stand and that the defendant had refused. To further complicate this point, Vahey became District Attorney Katzmann's law partner in 1924, a situation which implies that he may not have been totally committed to his client.

There was no discussion of Vanzetti's political beliefs at this first trial, nor were Sacco, Boda, or Orciani linked with the robbery. Vanzetti was found guilty and sentenced to twelve to fifteen years in prison at hard labor.

A year passed between the trial for the Bridgewater attempt and the joint trial of Sacco and Vanzetti for the South Braintree murders. During that time, Vanzetti was removed to the Chester state prison to begin serving his first sentence while Sacco was left in the Dedham county jail. The two men did not see each other during this time nor for more than a few weeks from the time of their joint trial to the weeks on death row before their executions. In a way, this first year was harder on Sacco. He was in the cleaner, less strict county jail, but he could do no work at all because prisoners who have not been convicted may not labor for the state. His days dragged by, and the active Sacco became restless and uneasy. Vanzetti had work to distract him; he had been assigned to the prison shop where automobile license plates were made.

For the most part, Sacco and Vanzetti both considered themselves to be alone and friendless. Vanzetti had called himself "nameless in a crowd of nameless ones." The two came to America separately in the same year, 1908. Vanzetti had been born in a village in the Piedmont, and from the age of fourteen, when he had been apprenticed to a baker, had led a wandering sort of existence. He held a number of different jobs, first in Italy and then in the United States.

They could hardly have chosen a worse year to emigrate to America. The country was in a state of depression and jobs were hard to find. In his autobiography, written in prison, Vanzetti wrote of this time: "How well I remember standing at the Battery, in lower New York, upon my arrival, alone, with a few poor belongings in the way of clothes, and very little money. . . . Where was I to go? What was I to do? Here was the promised land. The elevated rattled by and did not answer. The automobiles and the trolleys sped by, heedless of me."[3] His first job in New York was as a dishwasher, and he held a series of fairly menial tasks in a number of New England towns and cities before settling down in Massachusetts as a fish peddler.

When Sacco came to America, he had a more positive approach at once. He looked around him and decided to become a skilled worker in order to be sure of jobs and money. Within a few years he was a happy and contented husband and father.

Two issues would be disadvantages during the trial. First, the two men were avowed anarchists. While they claimed that theirs was a philosophical position of the nonviolent type, Galliani's group had definitely been suspected in the recent bombings. Second, and perhaps more damaging in 1920, both had run away to Mexico in 1917 to avoid the draft. They had done this under a misapprehension. Aliens—neither was a citizen—could not be made to serve in the American armed forces. The one act that made the two draft dodgers was that they had failed to register. Since they had done this and run away as well, they were sure to be looked upon unfavorably by the jury. After only a few weeks in Mexico each had come back, to remain more or less in hiding during the rest of the war.

During the year Sacco and Vanzetti waited, both prosecution and defense built their cases. Katzmann and his staff had the cooperation of the Justice Department in their investigation. The understanding apparently was that if the two Italians were found innocent of the murder charge there would still be enough evidence to get them deported under the criminal anarchy law. The Justice Department investigation was thorough. It is interesting to read the opinion of one of the investigators, Fred Weyand, in a signed deposition on the case:

From my investigation, combined with the investigation made by the other agents of the Department in Boston, I am convinced not only that the men had violated the Selective Service rules and regulations and evaded the draft, but that they were anarchists, and that they ought to have been deported. . . . But I am also thoroughly convinced, and always have been, and I believe it is and always has been the opinion of such Boston agents of the Department of Justice as had any knowledge of the subject, that these men had nothing whatever to do with the South Braintree murders, and that their conviction was the result of co-operation between the Boston agents of the Department of Justice and the District Attorney. It was the general opinion of the Boston Agents of the Department of Justice having knowledge of the affair that the South Braintree crime was committed by a gang of professional highwaymen.[4]

It is a widely held opinion that the worst move made by the defense was to engage Fred Moore as their chief counsel. Moore was a radical labor lawyer from California whose free and easy ways (during one very hot day in court he took his shoes off) only further antagonized Judge Thayer. Moore saw that the Sacco-Vanzetti case had potential far beyond the simple case of murder and robbery, serious though it might be. He undertook a careful publicity campaign, trying to get the story as much press coverage as possible. He also conducted a number of spectacular appeals for money with which to handle the defense. It seemed possible to turn this one case into an international rallying ground for radicals and intellectuals of all persuasions. Moore was always short of funds. Although he was given $150 a week for expenses, it never was enough. His great mistake occurred because he was so ambitious. The prosecution was willing to leave all reference to the defendants' anarchism out of the trial; Moore wanted Sacco and Vanzetti to become symbols of the class struggle. For him it was imperative that the point be raised. He succeeded in making the trial an arena for libertarian versus conservative views. But in doing so, he may have cost two men their lives.

The trial was held in Dedham, Massachusetts, a quiet town along the Charles River. Its courthouse, built in 1827, was a stately building with Greek columns and an attractive dome. Outside, elms and lindens were in full foliage, when on May 31, 1921, the trial of Sacco and Vanzetti for murder began.

Troops guarded the courthouse. Two of the defense lawyers, Thomas and Jeremiah McAnarney, brothers, were searched for concealed weapons before being allowed into the courthouse. The two defendants had been overjoyed to see one another again when they were brought together just before the trial. Now, each morning they were led out into the courtroom in handcuffs and put into "the cage", a short wire enclosure used for all persons accused of capital crimes.

That Thayer disliked the defendants, was sure they were guilty, and was antagonistic to their chief counsel was soon apparent. The McAnarney's were convinced he was prejudicing the jury against the defense. On the second day of the trial a lawyer named William G. Thompson, who replaced Moore as defense attorney some time after the verdict was reached, sat in the courtroom as observer. Afterward he told the brothers, "Your goose is cooked. You will never in the world get those men acquitted. The judge is going to convict these two and see that nothing gets into the record; he is going to keep the record straight and you have no chance."[5] And this opinion was reached before a word of testimony was heard. Judge Thayer also had a bad habit of talking about the trial out of court to his friends and acquaintances. After the conviction he told one of them, "Did you see what I did with those anarchist bastards?" Not only did he hate the men for being anarchists, but he seemed convinced they were guilty. After days spent in selecting jurors, the actual case began at the height of the hot Massachusetts summer.

There were only a few main points to the prosecution's case. First it was shown that the defendants had lied to the police on the night of their arrest. In rebuttal to this can be presented the fact that they were never told why they had been picked up and were sure they were going to be charged with criminal anarchy and wanted to protect their friends.

The prosecution showed that the two Italians had weapons on them for which they had no permit at the time of the arrest. The district attorney tried to establish that Vanzetti's gun had been taken from the body of Berardelli, the dead guard for whose murder they were on trial. It is true that no gun was found on Berardelli, but his wife wasn't sure he had one with him that day. A few days before the murder he had taken his in for repair. No record at the gunshop indicated it had been called for; but it was not in the shop. One of the repairmen testified that he had put a new hammer into Berardelli's gun and that Vanzetti's had a similar new hammer, but the point is confused and no real confirmation of the repairman's testimony was given. Apparently a check by serial number was not possible. Furthermore, no one had seen any of the bandits take anything from the body.

The prosecution implied that the other three men in the crime were Orciani, Boda, and Coacci, but none of these was on trial, nor were any of them ever indicted for the crime.

Eyewitnesses identified Sacco and Vanzetti as two of the South Braintree gang. Other eyewitnesses said they were sure the two were not among the five bandits.

A cap was found near the scene of the crime, and Sacco often wore caps. The prosecution claimed it was his. He tried it on and said it could not be his, it was too small for him. His wife said he never wore caps with earlaps, like the one found at the murder site. But when Sacco put his own cap on, it fit him as snugly as the one the prosecution presented in evidence, and Mr. Kelley, his boss, said he sometimes wore similar caps.

The prosecution showed that Sacco, who was a reliable worker, seldom was absent from the job, but that he did not come to work at the Three-K factory on April 15. Sacco presented rebuttal witnesses who remembered that he was in Boston on that day and that they saw him there. Sacco said that he had gone to the city to apply for a passport for his trip to Italy. In support of this there was proof that he had told the people at the plant that he planned to go to Boston sometime during that week to see about his passport. Later on the defense found a clerk at the consulate at that time who remembered that Sacco did come in that day. His recollection was so clear because the passport applicant had brought an out-of-size family portrait for the necessary photo that he and the others in the consulate had laughed about.

Vanzetti again claimed he had been selling fish. He remembered the day very well by this time because he had met a cloth peddler who had sold him a length of blue cloth for a new suit. The peddler, Joseph Rosen, testified for the defense, saying that he remembered the sale. Other witnesses stated they had seen him that day, but as the prosecution pointed out they were mostly friends of his.

The most substantial evidence, and the most disputed, was the testimony of ballistics experts for the defense and prosecution. The state's experts, in particular Captain William Proctor, seemed to believe that Sacco's gun had fired the fatal bullet into Berardelli. One of them, Charles Van Armburgh, continued to affirm this belief, but Proctor said later that that was not what his testimony meant at all. He had said under oath that the evidence was "consistent" with Sacco's gun having fired the fatal bullet, but he neglected to say, because he was not asked, that he himself believed that Sacco's gun was not the murder weapon.

Here, just as throughout the rest of the trial, contradictions abound. For example, the defense supplied its own expert, a man noted in the field, Albert Hamilton, who examined the Sacco gun after the verdict in the hope of finding enough evidence to warrant a new trial. For some reason, Hamilton had come to inspect the gun with two guns of his own. Judge Thayer grew suspicious and impounded Hamilton's guns before letting him leave. When Captain Van Armburgh made new tests he found that either accidentally or deliberately Hamilton had removed the barrel from Sacco's gun and switched it with one of his own. This discovery, of course, made his testimony worthless. Ironically, Van Armburgh was also discredited in connection with another case, where it was proved that he had tampered with the evidence.

In 1961 another series of ballistics tests was performed on Sacco's gun, and bullets fired from it were compared with the one removed from Berardelli's body. The ballistics experts used a modern comparison microscope for their tests. When the examination was over they declared that they were sure Sacco's gun had fired the murder bullet. If this was so, he would have been guilty of both robbery and murder.

Yet, after all these years, three possibilities still remain: the prosecution during the 1921 trial could have substituted a bullet fired from Sacco's gun for the real murder bullet; during the years the guns or bullets may have been mixed up and mismarked; Sacco may have had the gun and the gun may have been the murder weapon, but it could have been given to him after the crime by someone involved in it. A less likely possibility is that, because only one set of experts was involved, there may have been a mistake in their tests.

Finally, while this was never an issue at the trial, if Sacco and

Vanzetti were guilty of the robbery and murder what became of their share of the payroll money? None of it was ever found.

Sacco and Vanzetti were found guilty of murder in the first degree. Even after the verdict, some members of the prosecution had their doubts. When Thomas McAnarney stopped to congratulate the Assistant District Attorney Harold Williams on his victory, as is customary, Williams turned to him with tears in his eyes and said, "For God's sake, don't rub it in. This is the saddest thing that ever happened to me in my life."[6]

To this day no final, incontrovertible evidence has been produced by those who believe the two men guilty or by those who insist on their innocence. Judge Thayer was prejudiced against the anarchists, and the climate of opinion in the country was equally hostile. Yet, Thayer was known to be a man who kept his emotions out of the courtroom, and the recent ballistics evidence casts a doubt on Sacco's innocence; at the very least he probably knew who one member of the gang was. Carlo Tresca, a leading anarchist, said years later that he knew Sacco to be guilty and Vanzetti to be innocent. But he offered no proof. Francis Russell, the man who questioned Brini in 1961 and who conducted a long and thorough investigation of the case, came to the same conclusion in his book *Tragedy in Dedham*.

The case dragged on for six more years. Thompson took over the defense in 1923. Appeals were filed one after the other with Judge Thayer. He denied every one of them.

The strongest new evidence presented by the defense involved a series of confessions to the murder. As was usual after any trial, many persons confessed to the robbery and murder, but most of these could be discounted. But the ones involving the Joe Morelli gang have to be taken seriously. In 1923, Eric Moller, a Danish immigrant waiting deportation after being convicted on a criminal charge, asked to see Moore. He told the lawyer that he had been in the federal penitentiary in Atlanta with Joe Morelli, that Morelli often told him about crimes he had committed, and that the South Braintree robbery was one of them. According to Moller, Morelli told about the crime in detail. Perhaps Moller was telling the truth; perhaps he wanted money or a delay on his deportation.

For two years nothing further was done with this information. Then, on November 18, 1925, a trusty gave Sacco a magazine to read. In it was a note from Celestino Medeiros, a Portuguese gangster who had been convicted of a holdup murder. The note read: "I here by confess to being in the south Braintree shoe company crime and Sacco and Vanzetti was not in said crime."

Medeiros had been convicted for a robbery similar to the South Braintree one. He later signed an affadavit confessing to the crime and giving more details, but he was wrong in many of them. Again, the reason for the confession may not be obvious at once. Medeiros was known to be untruthful; he, too, may have wanted money from the defense fund. A stronger reason surely existed in the fact that he could not now be executed until a final decision was reached on the Sacco-Vanzetti appeals.

A man called Jimmy Weeks signed an affadavit stating that Medeiros told him that he had been a member of the South Braintree gang, and others were willing to say the same thing. Most important, in 1931, after the two men were executed, Joe Morelli said he and his gang had committed the robbery. But he would only sign a statement to this effect for a large sum of money. The money was never paid. In Morelli's unpublished autobiography is a statement about the crime. It may be the truth; it may have been written in anger because his demands for money were not met. At any rate, he wrote that his gang was supposed to do the job, but that Sacco, Vanzetti, Coacci, and Boda had double-crossed him and pulled off the crime a week early.

During all the appeals and gathering of evidence, Sacco and Vanzetti were waiting to die in prison. Sacco went on a hunger strike on February 14, 1923; it resulted in his being placed under observation and then committed to the Bridgewater State Hospital for the Criminally Insane on April 23. He was in the hospital five months before the doctors considered him well enough to be sent back to prison. Twenty-one months later Vanzetti was committed to the same institution and kept there for several months.

The waiting was over on April 23, 1927. In the Dedham courtroom on a sunny spring morning, Sacco and Vanzetti were sentenced to death by Judge Thayer. In the long speech he made before sentence was passed, Vanzetti said, "I am suffering because I am an Italian and indeed I am an Italian; I have suffered more for my family and for my beloved than for myself; but I am so convinced to be right that if you could execute me two times, and if I could be born two other times, I would live again to do what I have done already."[7]

Shortly before the sentencing, Felix Frankfurter, not yet a Supreme Court Justice, published a long article in the *Atlantic Monthly* called "The Case of Sacco and Vanzetti," which was later expanded and published as a book. Frankfurter whole-heartedly believed in the innocence of the two men, and his arguments on their behalf were very strong. This was the high point of a long campaign during 1927 to have the case re-evaluated. Speeches, articles, newspaper stories, poems, all were being turned out in large quantities and bore as their thesis belief in the innocence of Sacco and Vanzetti.

Numerous petitions and letters were sent to Governor Fuller requesting clemency, pardon, or a new trial. Most of these were never seen by the governor, but thrown out or filed away by his secretary, Herman MacDonald. Yet Fuller was in enough doubt to spend weeks studying the case on his own. Finally, on June 1, he appointed a three-man committee headed by the president of Harvard, Abbott Lawrence Lowell. The committee was to examine the evidence and give him its opinion on a course of action. The report given on July 27 said that there were no discrepancies or prejudices indicated in the trial record that would validate a new trial or a suspension of the death sentence. On August 3, Governor Fuller issued a statement that he would not set aside the death penalty.

Toward the end of the appeals, affadavits, and expectations that never materialized, Sacco lost faith and refused to associate himself with the defense any longer. When he was moved into death row, he awaited his execution stolidly. Vanzetti still had hope, or at any rate he would not stop fighting for his life. After the move to death row, bombs were exploded in a Philadelphia church and at the home of the mayor of Baltimore. It was assumed that this was a threat of violence to come if Sacco and Vanzetti were executed. As usual, the police never captured any of the bombers.

Sympathy for the two ran strong throughout Europe. In the last months protests were signed, speeches made, and petitions circulated. The Sacco-Vanzetti case was considered proof of American stupidity. The protests were joined in America by professors and college students as well as by a number of noted lawyers and judges.

At the very end the execution was delayed twelve days, from August 10 to August 22. But it was the final, doomed attempt at a reprieve. By the last day all the possible avenues of escape had been tried by the defense. Shortly after midnight on the 23rd, three executions were held. First came Medeiros, whose extra time had finally run out. He shrugged his shoulders and sat down in the electric chair, making no statement.

A protest demonstration against the death penalty for Sacco and Vanzetti

The Bettmann Archive

Sacco was then brought into the execution chamber. As he was being strapped into the electric chair he called out in Italian, "Long live anarchy!" Then, just as the switch was being pulled, "Farewell my wife and child and all my friends." To the witnesses he said, "Good evening, gentlemen," and then, "Farewell, Mother."

Vanzetti, the last to die, said, "I wish to say to you that I am innocent. I have never done a crime, some sins, but never any crime. I thank you for everything you have done for me. I am innocent of all crime, not only this one but of all, of all. I am an innocent man." Then, his last words, "I now wish to forgive some people for what they are doing to me."[8]

The Sacco and Vanzetti case did not end that night. Feeling was so strong that some 200,000 watched their funeral procession in which almost 7,000 persons marched.

Many writers of the day found their lives changed by this event. Edna St. Vincent Millay was a firm believer in their innocence. She wrote several poems about the case; in her "Justice Denied in Massachusetts," are the lines:

> Let us go home, and sit in the sitting-room
> Not in our day
> Shall the cloud go over and the sun rise as before . . .
> We shall not feel it again.
> We shall die in darkness and be buried in the rain.[9]

The case is still alive today. Opinion as to the guilt or innocence of the two executed men is still strongly divided. To some it is a terrible miscarriage of justice, to others it shows the power of the American courts. At any rate, the radical was placed in a more prominent position in America because of Sacco and Vanzetti, and the intellectuals united as a class for the first time in their defense.

Shortly after he was sentenced to death, Vanzetti was interviewed by a reporter, Philip D. Strong. He said:

If it had not been for this thing I might have lived out my life, talking at street corners to scorning men. I might have die, unmarked, unknown, a failure. Now we are not a failure. This is our career and our triumph. Never in our full life can we hope to do such work for tolerance, for justice, for man's understanding of man, as we now do by an accident.

Our words—our lives—our pains—nothing! The taking of our lives—lives of a good shoemaker and a poor fish peddler—all! That last moment belong to us—that agony is our triumph![10]

14

Anarchism in Modern Society

Until the last few years, "anarchism" in the United States was almost forgotten. The extremists of the left who have been regarded as dangerous since the 1930's have been the communists. But recently the word is coming back into use. For instance, in an article about an interview with him, Karl Shapiro, the noted American poet said:

> What I told him [the interviewer] finally was that I had no choice of candidates, that I do not vote (except on local matters) that I am opposed to voting under the "two party" system, and that I even attempt to spread a no-voting propaganda among my friends and students. . . .
>
> I had a distinct impression that my position or lack of it was quite familiar to my visitor. The word 'anarchism' did not come up in conversation, but we managed to discuss it without naming it.[1]

Even the title of Shapiro's article is significant: "On the Revival of Anarchism." And the revival he is speaking of occurs in the thought and actions of the young, the new college-age generation for the most part. The "hippies," in San Francisco and New York, who are disaffiliated, who have withdrawn from society, morality, and the economic norm of modern society to lead a life of emotional anarchy, are a part of this revival. So, to some extent, are the extreme wing of the Negro civil rights movement and the young ultra-conservatives whose hero is William Buckley or Robert Welch of the John Birch Society. But both of these groups are concerned with *achieving* political, social, and economic power, not with *eliminating* such power completely. The riots of the summer of 1967 are termed "rebellious," not an "urge to anarchy." Some deep uneasiness and restlessness have spread and are responsible for the new currency of anarchist thought. In his article, Shapiro goes on to say:

It is indeed our industrial way of life that lends sanction to militarism and colonialism. . . . Our enemy, strange as it may sound to American ears is the Standard of Living. . . . To lower this standard, or to equalize it among the peoples of the world, is our greatest need. And the first step is to disassociate ourselves from the industrial-scientific madness that rules our lives for twenty-four hours a day.[2]

Among the changes science has brought to everyone's life are an impersonality and rigidity caused by automation and the limitation of computer language, and—more seriously—the ability of the State to extend itself to supervision of every aspect of life. All the tools for this omnipotent "Big Brother" are at hand—sophisticated bugging devices that invisibly record or tap conversations on the phone, in rooms blocks away, or even between two persons walking down a street. Moreover, as the government completes its plans to computerize its knowledge of every tax-paying citizen, more information about each adult will be readily available to any government agency authorized to have it.

There is, too, a feeling of antagonism between humans and the machines that they have constructed. This has resulted in a growing sense of the human being as a machine and in an alienation from society and from emotion. Men feel a loneliness unique in Western civilization; they walk through their lives alone and loveless, with no desires or ambitions. That is the picture of alienated man expressed in literature and in psychology. The recent involvement with hallucinatory drugs, the need to "go on a trip," strongly implies that the "real" world is unsatisfactory.

Thus, a fear for the safety of mankind, a revulsion at man's growing lack of identity, and a desire to prevent the State from becoming all-powerful has led to a rebirth of anarchist thought, whether it is officially called by that name or not.

Again, it seems very doubtful whether an anarchistic society is the answer to these modern problems. In fact, such esteemed political commentators as Sebastian de Grazia find that this alienation from a political community, this *anomie*, is destructive to humanity and without correction could lead to the downfall of Western civilization. De Grazia identifies anomie with a lack of goals, with a feeling of restless anxiety. For him it has one central cause. The ruled have lost their sense of ruler and authority, which is tied to love and satisfaction. Only if men can again accept that somewhere there is a ruler (in both the political and religious sense) can they again joyously and fully partake of the political community.

As early as 1942 the noted sociologist Robert E. Park wrote: "Everywhere in the Great Society the relations of men, which were intimate and personal, have been more or less completely superseded by relations that are impersonal and formal. The result is that in the modern world in contrast with earlier and simpler societies, every aspect of life seems to be mechanized and radicalized. This is particularly true in our modern cities which are in consequence so largely inhabited today by lonely men and women."[3]

Certainly the young members of the New Left frequently speak of a need to re-establish "loving, interpersonal relationships." But they also have an aggressive lack of political philosophy; they have no program for future positive changes in society. They dissent but seldom construct a system that is to their satisfaction. De Grazia might interpret this to mean that they cannot maintain a healthy society, that they suffer from acute anomie.

The very fact that most of the new impetus to anarchy is a negative, critical impulse rather than an attempt to establish a Utopian society may be extremely valuable, for it is its criticism of present-day society that is anarchism's most useful contribution. That there is direct antigovernment action and that this action now frequently takes the form of civil disobedience is apparent. The burning of draft cards by young men who are pacifists, the sit-ins, lie-ins, and other violations of laws (whether or not they are morally right, they are laws) is a new assertion of the old anarchist theory that when law conflicts with morality, law must be disobeyed and a man must be true to what he knows to be ethically right.

Anarchism has another strong appeal at the present time. Its historical union with nonurban society is appealing at a time when huge cities are becoming unlivable. In the article mentioned earlier, Karl Shapiro wrote:

Any gradual and immediate diminution of our involvement with the industrial system, on any level, would have a direct effect on the peace and well-being of our people. To remove ourselves from the world of competition is of paramount importance to the individual and to the nation. Competition is the terrible vice of modern society.[4]

To replace competition, Shapiro would establish a way of life based on nonviolence, as taught by Mohandas Gandhi. It is opposed to the class war, the competition of industrialism, and the mutual hostility of governments, as well as to the State itself. Nonviolence, instead, is individual behavior, moral self-government by one man or a group of men—in short, a variation of Christian anarchism.

In 1966, Professor Irving Sarnoff, a psychologist, published a book, *Society with Tears*, which deals with the destructive nature of modern society and places in opposition to it a "humane society." Committed to the development and realization of human potential, the humane society—which he puts forth as a Utopia —would get rid of these three things: property, God, and the State, "the three concepts that have stimulated man's pursuit of limitless aggrandisement." The humane society would be a collectivist, nonauthoritarian community. Instead of aggrandisement, the desire for power, wealth, and prestige, the values of realization, of giving, and altruistic social concern would exist in the humane society.

Sarnoff is willing to accept in this Utopia the scientific advances developed in recent years. His economy would be automated, for example, but it would be entirely cooperative, with each man valued equally and receiving equal compensation for his labors. The few jobs remaining in the automated factories and service areas would not be held by men who specialized in one task, but by rotating groups of laborers who moved from job to job. When it would be necessary to specialize in one job, the specialists would be valued no more highly than anyone else in the society.

As modern anarchists realistically must, Sarnoff acknowledges that certain tasks of government—the arrival at, coordination of, and implementation of public policies—must be achieved. But he proposed that the unit of such organization should be small, personal groups of co-workers who would elect representatives to serve on councils and act as the entire group's voice. By extension, these local councils would then elect representatives to serve on larger ones, and so on, until the international level is reached. But this implies either unanimous consent or, again, the monopoly of the majority, which anarchists will not accept. There would, of couse, be no military, no weapons, for without the State the humane society would have no need of war—there would be no competition among national units.

Crime, too, in the Utopian, humane society would disappear, because the motivations of the criminal—private property, power, and advancement in the social scheme—would not exist. The only crimes would involve attempts to exploit other men or working for one's private gain. These would be "punished" by moral re-education.

Here is the problem with his plan, and Dr. Sarnoff recognizes this: granted the "humane society" is a reconciliation of the antistatism of the last century with the modernism of the present, still it is based on a belief that man is inherently perfectible, that he can willingly and universally lead a life dedicated to the good of others and to the fulfillment of himself as a creator at all levels of existence.

Dr. Sarnoff differs with those anarchists who have found the American pioneer to be a spiritual brother. He sees the frontiersman as one who is anxious to possess, who views the acres of virgin soil before him with greed, and who then defends what he has taken from any challengers.

This interpretation of the pioneer is a significant one. It illuminates the apparently paradoxical fact that the inheritors of the more simple, direct native American anarchism are not the communists and socialists of modern times, but rather the extreme conservatives.

The radical right's most pervasive program in the last twenty years has been a campaign against American foreign policy and against what it considers to be a serious amount of communist infiltration into American institutions. But these extreme conservatives also concern themselves with the domestic life of this country. Like those they oppose, the members of the radical right are discontented with many American institutions. They are suspicious of and unhappy with federal authority, and they have been unable to reconcile themselves to living in committed obedience to all laws and regulations. They, of course, would welcome the free society, in the sense that they are exponents of laissez-faire industrialism and opposed to government coercion when it comes to income taxes; laws regulating industry, working hours, and wages; social welfare legislation; and government inspection of foods, drugs, and other industrial products. Their opposition is purely self-interested in that they wish to have better conditions in which to make more money. But it must be remembered that the individualist anarchists also advocated egoism and taking all the power and goods one was allowed to take.

The radical rightists are perfectionists, too, just like the anti-statists. They believe either in perfect authority or in a perfect society where each man has the chance to get what he wants and to fight to hold onto what he has. Men should be as self-reliant as possible.

With remarkable inconsistency, the radical rightists insist on federal control of as rigid and extensive a nature as possible in one area: the control of, discovery of, and elimination of communists and communist sympathizers in this country. Most extreme conservatives do not realize that by wanting federal enforcement of projected laws in this area they are asking the government to control the very areas where they find objectionable forces. This desire to limit personal freedom arises in part because these persons do not accept the anarchist belief in the essential goodness of all human beings. Thus, the extreme rightists believe in a system of *economic* individual freedom, not in social and political personal liberty—that is, that each person should be able to choose his own actions in total liberty.

But the platform the radical rightists advocate nevertheless is directly connected to Benjamin Tucker's philosophy of individualist antistatism, and to that of all the other "scientific" anarchists.

Listen, for example, to Admiral Ben Moreell, who, in a 1963 speech, urged a return to the standards of the Founding Fathers, from which a man "derives directly from the Creator, his rights to life, to liberty, and to the unhampered use of his honestly acquired property. . . ." In an interview, the admiral said, "any effort to equalize the social and economic states of all individuals by the coercive power of government is a contradiction of nature's laws and can be achieved only by destroying individual freedom."[5]

Another time, the admiral said, "I stand with those who believe that the great conflict of our age is between Individualism and Collectivism, to determine whether the Individual, as a child of God and endowed by Him with certain inalienable rights, will be permitted to strive for a life in peaceful devotion to his God and in love of his neighbors; or, alternatively, whether his life is to be subordinated to the will of the majority."[6]

This can only be defined as economic anarchism. And the admiral is reinforced by many other extreme conservatives. Take, for example, a letter sent by Clarence Manion, a former law professor, to a number of business leaders:

The growing concentration of absolute power in the Federal Executive branch of our Government is destroying personal liberty, private property and private enterprise. The destruction is being accomplished through a spreading of unfathomable federal regulations and unlimited confiscatory taxes on all persons, all property, and every business enterprise.[7]

Manion insists that it is a violation of men's rights, for "each responsible human being has both a natural right and a natural duty to acquire and hold private property."

Probably the most noted speaker for the anarchist tendencies within the radical right is Ayn Rand, who is famous for her novels *The Fountainhead* and *Atlas Shrugged*. Born in St. Petersburg, Russia, in 1905, Miss Rand lived through the Russian Revolution and its aftermath in her country.[8] She now has an abhorrence of collectivism.

There does not seem to be any reference in Miss Rand's writings to the individualist American anarchists, but she has independently aligned herself with them. She often asserts the necessity of egoism. For example, her notes on *The Fountainhead* begin, "The first purpose of this book is a *defense of egoism in its real meaning*." The real meaning would seem to be not materialism—she dislikes the person who wants to work only to have more possessions or power than anyone else—but self-fulfillment and an honesty to what one believes. She also says of this book that it is "individualism vs. collectivism."

Just as she denies power and material greed, she cannot see any justification for a man wishing to rule over other men. Her first novel, *We the Living,* she said, was about "Man against the State." In *For the New Intellectual,* she goes on:

It requires the right to think and to act on the guidance of one's thinking—the right to live by one's own independent judgment. *Intellectual* freedom cannot exist without *political* freedom; political freedom cannot exist without *economic* freedom; *a free man and a free market are corollaries.*

The unprecedented social system whose fundamentals were established by the Founding Fathers, the system which set the terms, . . . was *capitalism.*

To be exact, it was not a full, perfect, totally unregulated *laissez-faire* capitalism. Various degrees of government interference and control still remained, even in America, as deadly cracks in the system's foundation.[9]

To the basic tenets of the individualist anarchists, she adds one more element—the anti-authoritarian society will be based on a capitalist economy. But this is not really a departure. Ayn Rand, like the extreme conservative, finds that society is essentially an economic construct. She says later in the same essay that the leader of the new society, the New Intellectual, will be a reunion of the intellectual and the businessman.

In one crucial passage in *The Fountainhead,* Miss Rand also advocated propaganda by deed. The novel's hero, Howard Roark, is a true egoist (in Miss Rand's sense). He is self-confident, interested not in altruism but in his own self-fulfillment. He is an architect and has designed a housing project for the lower classes. But the builders do not honor his plans. They keep his engineering plans but change the design of the buildings.

Roark dynamites the house and then waits to be arrested, planning to explain his act at his trial. There, he defends his move by denying the right of anyone to alter the achievement of a creatively independent mind (and by extension any one's achievement), and, in effect, epitomizes the struggle between individualism and collectivism. In a romantic conclusion, the jury frees him, dismissing the charges against him, thus vindicating the individual and heralding his triumph.

Equally unhappy with the present collectivist, impersonal state of American society are the members of the New Left. Most of them are students who were born at a time when the United States, newly conscious of its position as one of the two most important world powers, tried to shape international affairs and found that the world would not go its way. Democracy was not accepted eagerly by everyone to whom it was offered. The loss of China, the uneasy settlement of the Korean War, and the (to them) questionable ethics of the Vietnam conflict are hard to rationalize. Combined with the antagonism of some new African nations to what they regard as American imperialism, it has made these young men and women re-evaluate the United States' political system. With a certain amount of reason, they also express disillusionment with elected governmental officials. This is in part because for the first time newspapers, weekly news magazines, and television have revealed more of the governmental scandals from the State Department up to the highest authorities. Young men and women of the New Left are also critical of "managed" news and the obvious lack of candor sometimes indulged in by our highest officials.

This generation also bears the impact of the new collective American life style. The individualist, the eccentric genius who on his own makes a scientific breakthrough, is no longer the ideal American image. A man cannot make a million dollars by starting as a newsboy and working up to publisher of the world's largest newspaper; nor can he discover as complex a principle as that which inspired the laser or television all by himself; and if he could he could not afford to build his invention.

The trend now is toward scientific teams, toward medical group practice, toward corporate thinking. As the sociologist Daniel Bell has pointed out, these aggregates of humanity are today the units of social action, replacing the single-person unit of the past. Individual rights now in many cases are derived from group rights and in others seem to be identical with them.

So, the members of the Movement, as the New Left is some-times called, are suspicious of any political or economic or psychological or sociological orientation, because all of these use theories based on statistics—the final reduction of a mass of individuals to a few figures indicating "trends." They cannot find a modern philosophy of any type based on individual persons and their relations, hopefully loving and honest, with one another. If the anarchism of the radical right is economic, that of the New Left is of the soul.

These young persons reject the authority of both the conservatives and the liberals. They are nonaffiliated. And this often extends to a lack of affiliation to government and an unwillingness to obey laws and social customs. They find the modern, semi-automated, industrially polluted city depressing and unlivable and are alienated from it. In a desire to make their lives as simple as possible, and perhaps to emulate spiritual leaders such as Tolstoy and Gandhi, a number of the Movement's partisans have turned their backs on the wealth and luxuries of the new tech-nological age, preferring to limit their lives to the necessities of food, drink, and shelter.

This lack of affiliation, this desire for self-fulfillment and moral behavior (based on personal morality, or its lack, only) has enabled these New Leftists to be activists. They feel no qualms at basing a civil rights movement on greater or lesser civil diso-bedience; the draft card burner is more respected than the law he is breaking. But for all their political agitation most of the New Left (except for declared communists and socialists) have no political platform at all. Their interest focuses on *society* and making it better for men to live in rather than on government and the State. If they are affiliated to anything, it is to all the individuals in the world and to finding each a proper place in society and a share in its decisions.

Most of the members of the SDS (Students for a Democratic Society), for example, are unwilling even to think in terms of *theory* or *ideology*, both of which they find suspicious and unpleasant words. In writing about the SDS, two commentators note that leadership, traditional authority, and arbitrary decision-making have no place in the organization. One SDS member said, in effect, that "Leaders mean organization, organization means hierarchy, and hierarchy is undemocratic. It connotes bureaucracy and impersonality."[10]

While anarchism as a political doctrine may have few avowed adherents in the 1960's it would seem apparent that anarchist ideas have pervaded social thought on both extremes of the political spectrum. There are, too, still philosophical anarchists trying to formulate a workable position for this time. The most famous American antistatist is Paul Goodman, writer, teacher, and social critic. He has taught courses in the methods of group therapy and in other aspects of psychology at several universities; he has also written several volumes of poetry and fiction and thinks of himself as an artist who through his art is trying to reshape anarchism. In his redefinition of key anarchist concepts, he has written:

In my opinion we must understand freedom in a very positive sense: it is the *condition of initiating* activity. Apart from this pregnant meaning, mere freedom from interference is both trivial and *in fact cannot be substantially protected*. For even while persons feel themselves inviolate in their bodies, their rights, their families, etc., they are effectually hemmed in, imposed upon, and their resources for action pre-empted. (In my opinion we are hastening rapidly into an American fascism-of-the-majority of just that kind; a couple of bad reverses and the brutality of it will appear.[11]

He considers civil disobedience of an idealistic nature—for example that practiced by the Committee for Nonviolent Action, or of those who demonstrate for peace and refuse the draft—sensible antiauthoritarian activism. Indifference and unconcerned behavior are crimes, acts of treason against natural society. Thus men say the system is guilty, but the system is made of men, who if they disapprove of it can leave it or fight it.

In 1945, in *Drawing the Line*, Goodman pointed out to those in the libertarian movement that they were taking stands on already outmoded issues. For him, "acts which in fact rouse a coercive reaction have libertarian force."[12] Goodman then points out that some acts are crimes in a natural society, but some, on the other hand, undermine the present coercive society and in it are considered "crimes," while in a natural one they would not be thought of in this way. He then urges sympathy with, or practice of—depending on the individual's conscience and inclinations—"acts of liberty," which modern society may consider "antisocial."

His chief interest is in the creation of a livable environment for human individuals. So he advocates the traditional anarchist stand in favor of decentralization and envisions a society of small, decision-making centers in which the members voluntarily cooperate. Even in a large city, the existence of which Goodman must accept if he is not to confine his ideas to the purely theoretical, there could be a local city hall for each neighborhood, and all the persons in the neighborhood could have a voice in the function of their transportation, schools, sanitation, and health services without intereference from the State.

Similarly, Goodman suggests universities operating as independent, self-governing units within which there would exist self-governing student organizations that would have a voice in school problems and policies. These quasi-anarchist universities would be small and locally structured, and they would replace such educational monoliths as the University of California where only recently the students vigorously demonstrated for self-government and freedom of expression.

Few of us would willingly turn back the clock several centuries. We must face the complexities and characteristics of society as it exists. Along with the evils have come benefits, such as medical improvements, higher standards of living, longer life expectancies, that it would be foolhardy to wish away. With daily increases in population, future food shortages, and the multiple social and economic problems created by technology and industrialization, it does not seem possible that man will ever be able to do without some regulatory agencies.

Although a world without law, government, and coercive behavior in which each man lived a morally oriented life is tempting, it is probably an ideal that can never be achieved. Like closet drama, the play meant to be read rather than performed, it is romantically appealing with little practical value.

Yet society as it exists today is far from perfect. The anarchist is basically an optimist, and he is an acute social and political critic. More important, anarchism now is the most concentrated spokesman for the importance of individual liberty and the necessity for a man to rule his own life. The modern world needs to hear that voice.

Not until the world is acceptable to every person living in it, not until each one of us is fulfilling his potentialities completely, not until each man has a voice in his own future, will anarchist thought no longer be necessary.

Reference Notes

CHAPTER 1

1. Woodcock, George, *Anarchism: A History of Libertarian Ideas and Movements*. Cleveland and New York: The World Publishing Company (Meridian Books), 1962, p. 41.

CHAPTER 2

1. *Encyclopedia of the Social Sciences*. New York: The Macmillan Company 1930, Vol. I.
2. Woodcock, *op. cit.*, p. 41.
3. Turner, Frederick Jackson, *The Frontier in American History*. New York: Henry Holt and Company, 1920, pp. 61–62

CHAPTER 3

1. Schuster, Eunice Minette, "Native American Anarchism: A Study of Left-Wing American Individualism," *Smith College Studies in History,* Vol. XVII (October 1931–July 1932) Nos. 1–4, p. 20.
2. *Ibid.*
3. Parrington, Vernon Louis, *Main Currents in American Thought*. New York: Harcourt, Brace and Company, 1930.
4. *Ibid.,* p. 143.
5. *Ibid.,* pp. 144–45.
6. Tocqueville, Alexis de, *Democracy in America*. New York: Alfred A. Knopf (Vintage Books), 1954, Vol. I, p. 31.

CHAPTER 4

1. Parrington, *op. cit.,* p. 238.
2. De Cleyre, Voltarine, *Anarchism and American Traditions*. Chicago: Free Society Group, 1922, p. 345.
3. Paine, Thomas, *Common Sense*. London: W. T. Sherwin, 1817, p. 5.
4. Halévy, Elie, *The Growth of Philosophical Radicalism*. London: Faber and Faber Ltd., 1927, p. 190.
5. *Ibid.*
6. Beard, Charles A. *The Myth of Rugged American Individualism*. New York: The John Day Company, 1932, p. 21.
7. De Cleyre, *op. cit.,* p. 349.

8. Rocker, Rudolf, *Pioneers of American Freedom*. Los Angeles: Rocker Publications Committee, 1949, p. 14.
9. *Ibid.*, p. 13.
10. Beard, *op. cit.*, p. 21.
11. Rocker, *op. cit.*, p. 14.

CHAPTER 5

1. Parks, Henry Banford, "Introduction," in William Alfred Hinds, *American Communities*. New York: Corinth Books (The American Experience Series), 1961, (1st pub., 1878), p. *v*.
2. Tocqueville, *op cit.*, Vol. II, p. 304.
3. *Ibid.*, Vol II, p. 130.
4. *Ibid.*, Vol. II, p. 104.
5. *Ibid.*, Vol. II, p. 106.
6. *Ibid.*, Vol. I, p. 42.
7. *Ibid.*, Vol. I, p. 62.
8. *Ibid.*, Vol. II, pp. 304–05.
9. Parrington, *op. cit.*, p. 390.
10. Woodcock, *op. cit.*, p. 454.
11. Rocker, *op. cit.*, p. 23.
12. Emerson, Ralph Waldo, *Journals of Ralph Waldo Emerson, with*
13. Parrington, *op. cit.*, p. 405.
    Annotations. Boston, Houghton Mifflin, 1909–14, Vol. IV, p. 242.
14. Blau, Joseph L., *Men and Movements in American Philosophy*. New York: Prentice-Hall, 1952, p. 134.
15. Parrington, *op. cit.*, p. 409.
16. Thoreau, Henry David, *Works*. Boston, Houghton Mifflin, 1894, Vol. X, p. 131.
17. *Ibid.*
18. Rocker, *op. cit.*, p. 157.
19. Osgood, Herbert L., "Scientific Anarchism," *Political Science Quarterly*, Vol. IV (March 1889) No. 1, p. 3.
20. Day, Dorothy, *The Long Loneliness*, New York: Harper & Bros., 1931, p. 185.
21. Nordhoff, Charles, *The Communistic Societies of the United States*. New York: Hilary House Publishers, Ltd., 1960 (1st pub. 1875), p. 12.
22. Brogan, D. W., *The American Character*. New York: Alfred A. Knopf, 1944 (reprinted by Time, Incorporated), p. 19.

CHAPTER 6

1. Warren, Josiah, *Periodical Letter,* II (July 1856), pp. 55–56.
2. Warren, Josiah, *Practical Details. . . .* New York, 1852, p. 13.

3. Horowitz, Irving L., ed., *The Anarchists*. New York: Dell Publishing Company, Inc., 1964, p. 322.
4. Warren, Josiah, *True Civilization* . . . Boston, 1863, p. 74.
5. Martin, James Joseph, *Individualist Anarchism in the United States*. Unpublished Ph.D. thesis, 1949, p. 133.
6. Rocker, *op. cit.*
7. Martin, *op. cit.*
8. Rocker, *op. cit.*, p. 65.
9. Warren, *True Civilization,* op. cit., p. 126.
10. *Ibid.*, p. 125.

CHAPTER 7

1. Carr, Edward Hallet, *Studies in Revolution*. New York: Barnes & Noble, Inc., 1962, p. 47.
2. Heilbroner, Robert L., *The Worldly Philosophers*. New York: Simon & Schuster, 1953, 1961 (reprinted in Time Reading Program, 1962), pp.129–30.
3. Spencer, Herbert, *Social Statics* q.v. in Gladden, Washington, "The Philosophy of Anarchism" *Outlook*. Vol. 69 (Oct. 19, 1901) No. 7, p. 452.
4. Horowitz, *op. cit.*, pp. 291–92.
5. Krimerman, Leonard I., and Perry, Lewis, *Patterns of Anarchy*, Garden City, N.Y.: Doubleday & Co., 1966, pp. 181–82.
6. *Ibid.*, p. 179.

CHAPTER 8

1. Channing, William Ellery, *Works*. Boston, Vol. II.
2. *Ibid.*, Vol. II, p. 44.
3. *Ibid.*, Vol. II, p. 27.
4. Garrison, William Lloyd, *Life of William Lloyd Garrison*. Boston, The Anti-Slavery Office, 1845, pp. 145–48 *passim*.
5. Krimerman and Perry, *op. cit.*, p. 143.
6. Rocker, *op. cit.*, p. 36.
7. Schuster, *op. cit.*, pp. 148–49.
8. Spooner, Lysander, *Poverty: Its Illegal Causes and Legal Cure.* Boston, B. Marsh, 1846, p. 59.
9. Krimerman and Perry, *op. cit.*, p. 243.
10. *Ibid.*
11. *Ibid.*, p. 246.
12. Trowbridge, John T., "A Reminiscence of the Pantarch," *The Independent,* Vol. LV (February 26, 1903), p. 499.
13. Martin, *op. cit.*, p. 310.
14. Schuster, *op. cit.*, p. 129.

15. Heywood, Ezra, ed., *Declaration of Sentiments and Constitution of the New England Labor Reform League.* Boston, 1869, p. 6.

CHAPTER 9

1. Heywood, Ezra, *The Word.* I, (May, 1872), p. 3.
2. Greene, William B., *Equality.* West Brookfield, Mass., 1849, pp. 70–71.
3. Adamic, Louis, *Dynamite, the Story of Class Violence in America.* New York: The Viking Press, 2nd ed., 1934, p. 47.
4. David, Henry, *The History of the Haymarket Affair.* New York: Collier Books, 1963 (1st pub. 1936), p. 86.
5. *Ibid.*, p. 95.
6. *Ibid.*, p. 96.
7. Yellen, Samuel, "American Propagandists of the Deed," in Krimerman and Perry, *op. cit.*, p. 423.

CHAPTER 10

1. David, *op. cit.*, pp. 112–13.
2. *Ibid.*, pp. 160–61.
3. *Ibid.*, p. 176.
4. *Ibid.*
5. *The New York Times,* Vol. XXXV, No. 10, 818, p. 1.
6. Altgeld, John Peter, *The Mind and Spirit of John Peter Altgeld.* Urbana, Ill.: University of Illinois Press, 1965, pp. 95–96.
7. Yellen, *op. cit.*, p. 430.
8. David, *op. cit.*, p. 204.
9. *Ibid.*, p. 216.
10. Altgeld, *op. cit.*, p. 95.
11. David, *op. cit.*, p. 240.
12. *Ibid.*, pp. 290–91.
13. *Ibid.*, p. 387.

CHAPTER 11

1. De Cleyre, Voltarine, "Why I am an Anarchist," *Mother Earth,* Vol. 3 (March 1908), No. 1, p. 16.
2. *Ibid.*, p. 7.
3. Gladden, *op. cit.*, p. 450.
4. Sachs, Emanie, *The Terrible Siren.* New York: Harper & Bros., 1928, p. 242.
5. Commons, John R., quoted in Eltzbacher, Paul, *Anarchism.* New York: Libertarian Book Club, 1960.
6. Tucker, Benjamin, *Liberty.* Vol. I (Sept. 7, 1881), p. 2.
7. Eltzbacher, *op. cit.*

8. Tucker, Benjamin, *Liberty*. Vol. V. (June 9, 1888), p. 5.
9. *Ibid.*, January 28, 1888, p. 5.
10. Tucker, Benjamin, *Instead of a Book, By a Man Too Busy to Write One*. New York, 1893, p. 143.
11. Madison, Charles A. "Benjamin Tucker: Individualist and Anarchist," *New England Quarterly*, Vol. XVI (September 1943) No. 3, p. 465.
12. Wood, Charles Erskine Scott, *Too Much Government*. New York: Vanguard Press, 1931, p. 166.

CHAPTER 12

1. Goldman, Emma, *Living My Life*. New York: Alfred A. Knopf, 1931, Vol. I, p. 5.
2. Tucker, Benjamin, *Liberty*. VII (July 30, 1892), p. 2.
3. Goldman, *op. cit.*
4. *Ibid.*, Vol. II, p. 296.
5. Baginski, Max, "Leon Czolgosz," *Mother Earth*, Vol. I (October 1906), No. 8, p. 9.
6. Reitman, Benjamin, "Emma Goldman on Tour in Chicago and San Francisco in 1908," *Mother Earth*, April-June 1908, p. 37.
7. *Ibid.*
8. House Committee on Immigration and Naturalization. Sixty-sixth Congress, Second Session. *Communist and Anarchist Deportation Cases. Digest of Cases Deported on U.S. Transport "Buford."* Washington, D.C.: Government Printing Office, 1920.
9. New York State Seditious Activities, Joint Legislative Committee to Investigate. *Preliminary Report and Recommendations.* Albany: J. B. Lyon Co., Printers, 1920, Vol. I, pp. 854–55.
10. Goldman, Emma and Berkman, Alexander, *Trial and Speeches of Emma Goldman and Alexander Berkman*. New York: Mother Earth Publishing Co., 1917, p. 89.
11. Murray, Robert K., *Red Scare*. New York: McGraw-Hill Book Co., 1964 (1st pub., 1955), p. 7.
12. *Statutes at Large*. Washington, D.C.: Government Printing Office, Vol. XL, p. 553.
13. House Committee on the Judiciary, Sixty-Sixth Congress, Second Session. *Sedition, Syndicalism, Sabotage, and Anarchy*. Washington, D.C.: Government Printing Office, 1920, p. 167.
14. Murray, *op. cit.*, p. 72.
15. House, 66:2, *Sedition, op. cit.*, p. 9.
16. *Ibid.*, p. 143.
17. Murray, *op. cit.*, pp. 182–84.
18. House, 66:2, *Buford, op. cit.*, pp. 91–93.

CHAPTER 13

1. Russell, Francis, *Tragedy In Dedham*: *The Story of the Sacco-Vanzetti Case*. New York: McGraw-Hill, 1962, pp. 63–64.
2. *Ibid.*, pp. 66–67.
3. *Ibid.*, p. 75.
4. *Ibid.*, pp. 122–23.
5. *Ibid.*, p. 133.
6. *Ibid.*, p. 215.
7. Weeks, Robert P., ed., *Commonwealth vs. Sacco and Vanzetti*. Englewood Cliffs, N.J.: Prentice-Hall, Inc., 1958, p. 223.
8. Russell, *op. cit.*, p. 450.
9. Millay, Edna St. Vincent, *Collected Lyrics of*. New York and London: Harper & Bros., Publishers, 1939, pp. 230–31.
10. Weeks, *op. cit.*, p. 226. Spelling changed by C. J.

CHAPTER 14

1. Shapiro, Karl, "On the Revival of Anarchism," *Liberation*. February 1961. In Horowitz, *op. cit.*, p. 573.
2. *Ibid.*, p. 574.
3. De Grazia, Sebastian, *The Political Community: A Study of Anomie*. Chicago: University of Chicago Press, 1963 (1st pub. 1948), p. 107.
4. Shapiro, *op. cit.*, p. 579.
5. Forster, Arnold, and Epstein, Benjamin R., *Danger on the Right*. New York: Random House, 1964, p. 180.
6. *Ibid.*, p. 183.
7. *Ibid.*, pp. 122, 125.
8. Branden, Barbara, "Who Is Ayn Rand?" in Nathaniel Branden, *Who Is Ayn Rand?* New York: Paperback Library, Inc., 1964, p. 126.
9. Rand, Ayn. *For the New Intellectual*. New York: New American Library (Signet Books), 1961 p. 25.
10. Jacobs, Paul, and Landau, Saul, *The New Radicals: A Report with Documents*. New York: Random House (Vintage Books), 1966, p. 31.
11. Krimerman and Perry, *op. cit.*, p. 55.
12. Goodman, Paul, *Drawing the Line*. New York: Random House, 1946, 1962, p. 20.

Significant Events in
The History of American Antistatism

1634   Anne Hutchinson and her husband arrive in Boston from England: The Massachusetts Bay Company begins representative government.

1635   Roger Williams is banished from Massachusetts colony after preaching the separation of church and state.

1636   Henry Vane, a supporter of the Antinomians, is elected Governor of Massachusetts.

1637   John Wheelwright delivers a sermon opposing fasts and asserting the sovereignty of the Elect above law and government; he is tried and convicted of sedition; Henry Vane is defeated in his campaign for Governor, and John Winthrop is re-elected Governor; Anne Hutchinson is tried for heresy. Massachusetts Colony enacts the first alien exclusion act.

1638   Anne Hutchinson is banished from Massachusetts; she settles on Aquidneck Island in Rhode Island with some of her followers.

1729   Benjamin Franklin's *A Modest Inquiry into the Nature and Necessity of Paper Currency* is published in Philadelphia.

1740   First American land bank.

1765   Stamp Act becomes law to raise more revenue from colonies; Sons of Liberty organized to resist enforcement of the Act.

1767   Townshend Revenue Act and Tea Act go into effect; colonial taxation is increased.

1773   Italian immigrants and materials used to begin silkworm culture in Virginia (later spreads to New Jersey).

1774   Thomas Jefferson's *Summary View of the Rights of British America . . .* is published; Rhode Island and Connecticut ban the importation of slaves; First Continental Congress; Thomas Paine, encouraged by Franklin, arrives in Philadelphia.

1775   First abolitionist society in America organized in Pennsylvania; Beginning of War for Independence.

1776   Paine publishes *Common Sense*; Declaration of Independence adopted by Congress.

1781   General Washington successful; Britain defeated and colonies achieve independence.

1782   Crevecoeur publishes *Letters from an American Farmer;* the Great Seal of the United States is adopted by Congress.

1783   Congress formally declares the end of the war.

1787   Constitutional convention held; the Federalist essays appear.

1789   George Washington and John Adams elected first President and Vice President of the United States; French Revolution begins.

1790   Congress receives first petitions to abolish slavery.

1791   Paine publishes *The Rights of Man.*

1792   First appearance of political parties in the United States: Federalists and Republicans.

1793   William Godwin publishes *Enquiry Concerning Political Justice* in England; France goes to war with England.

1794   First part of Paine's *The Age of Reason* is published in Paris.

1796   Godwin's *Political Justice* published in Philadelphia.

1798   Sedition Act punishes criticism of government.

1807   Congress prohibits bringing in any more slaves.

1812   United States goes to war with Britain; William Ellery Channing preaches his first anti-war sermon.

1814   Peace treaty signed with Britain.

1815   First peace society founded in New York with David Low Dodge as its president; Massachusetts Peace Society founded by Rev. Noah Worcester; peace concluded with Britain.

1826   Josiah Warren joins New Harmony.

1827   Warren starts his first Time Store.

1831   William Lloyd Garrison begins publication of *The Liberator.*

1832   Beginning of the New England Anti-Slavery Society.

1833   Warren begins to issue *The Peaceful Revolutionist,* the first anarchist newspaper.

1834   John Humphrey Noyes issues the first number of *The Perfectionist.*

1835   Alexis de Tocqueville publishes *Democracy in America*; Channing publishes *Slavery*, his first anti-slavery tract; Warren founds the Village of Equity.

1837   The New England Non-Resistant Society is formed; the American Peace Society says no war (defensive or offensive) is justifiable.

1838   *The Non-Resistant* begins publication.

1840   Pierre Joseph Proudhon's *What is Property?* is published in France.

1843   Lysander Spooner's agitation against slavery results in his having to leave Houston.

1844   Spooner starts the American Letter Mail Company.

1845   Max Stirner publishes *The Ego and His Own*; annexation of Texas.

1846   Warren publishes *Equitable Commerce;* Spooner publishes *The Unconstitutionality of Slavery*; Mexican-American War begins.

1847   Warren establishes Utopia in Ohio and reissues the *Peaceful Anarchist*; treaty with Mexico.

1848   Large German and French emigration to the United States because of the failure of their revolutions; beginnings of "Forty-Eighters" group; Warren moves to Boston; under the leadership of Noyes the Perfectionist community of Oneida is founded in New York State.

1849   William B. Greene publishes *Equality*; Henry David Thoreau's "On the Duty of Civil Disobedience" appears.

1850   Herbert Spencer's *Social Statics* is published in England; the Utopian anarchist community of Modern Times is established on Long Island; Greene publishes *Mutual Banking*; Fugitive Slave Act is passed by Congress, requiring the return to owners of escaped slaves.

1851   Karl Marx's *Revolution and Counter Revolution* is issued in installments by the New York *Tribune* (till 1852).

1852   Stephen Pearl Andrews publishes *The Science of Society*.

1853   Greene pleads for women's rights before the Massachusetts Constitutional Convention.

1854   Garrison publicly burns the Fugitive Slave Law and the Constitution; Warren begins to issue a monthly *Periodical Letter* from Modern Times.

1858   Joseph Dejacque begins to issue *Le Libertaire* in New York— the first foreign language anarchist paper in the United States.

1860   South Carolina secedes from the Union.

1861   The Civil War begins.

1864   The First International Working Men's Association founded.

1865   The South surrenders; Civil War over; Lincoln assassinated.

1867   Spooner publishes *No Treason;* Marx's *Das Kapital* is published.

1869   Ezra Heywood publishes *Yours or Mine*; the New England Labor Reform League is founded; Warren publishes *True Civilization*.

1871   American Labor Reform League begins.

1872   Heywood begins publication of his periodical *The Word*; the anarchists leave the International, unable to in any way control its policies.

1873   Benjamin Tucker meets Victoria Woodhull.

1875   Tucker joins Heywood on *The Word*; an armed working men's association begins to meet in Chicago.

1877   Tucker issues the short-lived *Radical Review*.

1878   Heywood is arrested and sentenced to two years in prison for the publication of obscene materials.

1881   The first issue of Tucker's *Liberty* appears; a decade of labor unrest begins in which 23,800 strikes and lockouts are recorded; the anarchist Black International meets in Chicago and the International Working People's Association is founded.

1882   Johann Most emigrates to the United States; Spooner publishes his *Letter to Thomas F. Bayard*.

1883   Most urges people to "propaganda by deed"; Albert Parsons begins to issue *The Alarm* in Chicago; the anarchist Pittsburgh congress meets.

1884   The anarcho-syndicalist Central Labor Union is formed.

1885   T. Lizius writes the famous "Dynamite" letter published in *The Alarm*; Emma Goldman emigrates to the United States.

1886   The Haymarket riot.

1887   Lingg commits suicide; Parsons, Spies, Fischer, and Engel executed.

1889   Anarchists join the Second International.

1890   Heywood again sentenced to two years in prison.

1892   Tucker begins to issue libertarian books in New York; Alexander Berkman attempts to assassinate Henry Clay Frick.

1893   Governor Altgeld pardons the three surviving anarchists convicted in the Haymarket affair: Neebe, Schwab, and Fielden; Tucker publishes *Instead of a Book*; Emma Goldman is sentenced to prison for one year for inciting to violence; stock market crash is followed by a four-year depression.

Significant Events in The History of American Antistation

1894   Congress passes a law prohibiting foreign anarchists admission to the United States.

1896   The anarchists are ejected from the London Congress of the Second International.

1897   The anarchist Home Colony is founded in Washington.

1898   Spanish-American War.

1899   Enrico Malatesta delivers a series of lectures on anarchism to Italian immigrants in New York; Thorstein Veblen publishes the *Theory of the Leisure Class.*

1900   Bresci assassinates King Humbert of Italy.

1901   Leon Czolgosz assassinates President McKinley.

1903   New laws are passed to exclude anarchists and radicals from the United States.

1905   The International Workers of the World is founded.

1906   The New York State criminal anarchy law is passed; Emma Goldman starts to issue *Mother Earth.*

1907   Tucker opens his libertarian bookstore.

1908   Tucker's stock, press, and manuscripts are destroyed by fire; the I.W.W. divides into two factions.

1917   United States enters World War I; Russian Revolution, United States first nation to recognize new government (refuses recognition after Bolsheviks take over); Espionage Act makes it illegal to obstruct the war effort in any way; Emma Goldman, Berkman, and others convicted on violations of the Espionage Act.

1918   End of World War I; 100 I.W.W. leaders convicted of conspiring against the American war effort (sentenced in 1920).

1919   Bombs are mailed to a number of conservatives (anarchists are believed responsible); Lusk Committee hearings begin in New York; Palmer raids begin on anarchist and radical organizations; the Communist Party holds its first American convention in Chicago; 249 aliens deported on the U.S.S. *Buford.*

1920   Sacco and Vanzetti arrested and tried for the South Braintree hold-up murders.

1927   Sacco and Vanzetti executed.

1929   The U.S. Supreme Court upholds the refusal of citizenship to an immigrant, Rosika Schwimmer, who is a pacifist; the stock market collapses and the depression begins.

1931   Charles Erskine Scott Wood publishes *Too Much Government.*

1933   Increased governmental regulations to alleviate depression marks a new trend in American government; the *Catholic Worker* is founded under the leadership of Dorothy Day.

1941   United States enters World War II.

1945   World War II ended with surrender of Germany and Japan; Paul Goodman publishes *Drawing the Line*; great labor unrest follows the peace.

1950   Korean War begins.

1953   Armistice reached in Korean War.

1960   Sit-ins begin as weapon of the civil rights movement, the "New Left" begins to function; SNCC organized.

1961   New ballistics evidence indicates that Sacco did have the murder weapon in his possession at the time of his arrest; his innocence is doubtful.

1962   SDS founded.

1965   20,000 march to Washington to protest the war in Vietnam; Congress enacts a law making the burning of a draft card punishable by five years in jail and a $5,000 fine; William Epton is convicted under New York's criminal anarchy law.

1966   Attempts are made in Congress to make all anti-war protests illegal.

1967   Anti-Viet Nam war protests continue; a number of books on the New Left and radical right achieve prominence.

Bibliography

At the present time there are no books in print dealing with the history of anarchism in America. Two earlier works, have discussed thoroughly and with great scholarship individualist anarchism in this country. They have been invaluable in the writing of this book:

Martin, James J. *Individualist Anarchism in the United States.* University of Michigan, Unpublished Ph.D. Thesis, 1949.

Schuster, Eunice Minette, "Native America Anarchism: A Study of Left-Wing American Individualism," *Smith College Studies in History.* Vol. XVII, Nos. 1–4 (October 1931–July 1932).

The books that follow are more specific, dealing with a particular section of the libertarian movement in America. I have not attempted to list any texts of anarchist theory other than some individualist documents.

Adamic, Louis. *Dynamite, the Story of Class Violence in America.* New York: The Viking Press, 2nd ed., 1934.

Andrews, Stephen Pearl. *The Science of Society.* New York: Fowler & Wells, 1852.

Billington, Ray Allen, and James Blaine Hedges. *Westward Expansion, a History of the American Frontier.* New York: The Macmillan Company, 1949.

Brogan, D. W. *The American Character.* New York: Alfred A. Knopf, Inc., 1944.

David, Henry. *The History of the Haymarket Affair.* New York: Collier Books, 1963.

De Cleyre, Voltarine. *Anarchism and American Traditions.* Chicago: Free Society Group, 1922.

De Grazia, Sebastian. *The Political Community: a Study of Anomie.* University of Chicago Press, 1948.

Felix, David. *Protest: Sacco–Vanzetti and the Intellectuals.* Bloomington, Ind., and London: Indiana University Press, 1965.

Goldman, Emma. *Living My Life.* New York: Alfred Knopf, Inc., 1931, 2 vols.

Goodman, Paul. *The Community of Scholars.* New York: Random House, 1962.

_____. *Drawing The Line.* New York: Random House, 1962.

_____. *People or Personnel.* New York: Random House, 1965.

Greene, William Bradford. *Equality.* West Brookfield, Mass., 1849.

_____ *Mutual Banking.* West Brookfield, Mass., 1850.

Halévy, Elie. *The Growth of Philosophical Radicalism.* Trans. Mary Morris. London: Faber & Faber Ltd., 1927.

Heilbroner, Robert L. *The Worldly Philosophers.* New York: Simon & Shuster, 1953, 1961.

Horowitz, Irving, ed. *The Anarchists.* New York: Dell Publishing Co., Inc., 1964.

Jacobs, Paul, and Saul Landau. *The New Radicals.* New York: Random House (Vintage Books) 1966.

Joll, James. *The Anarchists.* Boston: Little, Brown & Co., 1964.

Krimerman, Leonard I., and Lewis Perry. *Patterns of Anarchy.* Garden City, N.Y.: Doubleday & Co., 1966.

Miller, Michael V. and Susan Gilmore, eds. *Revolution at Berkeley.* New York: Dell Publishing Company, 1964.

Murray, Robert K. *Red Scare.* New York: McGraw-Hill, 1964.

Nordhoff, Charles. *The Communistic Societies of the United States.* New York: Hilary House Publishers, Ltd., 1960.

Paine, Thomas. *Common Sense,* London: W. T. Sherwin, 1817 (there are many later editions).

Parrington, Vernon Louis. *Main Currents in American Thought.* New York: Harcourt, Brace & Company, 1930.

Russell, Bertrand. *Proposed Roads to Freedom.* New York: Henry Holt & Company, 1919.

Russell, Francis. *Tragedy in Dedham: The Story of the Sacco–Vanzetti Case.* McGraw-Hill, 1962.

Sarnoff, Irving. *Society with Tears.* New York: The Citadel Press, 1966.

Thoreau, Henry David. *On Civil Disobedience.* There are many editions of this work.

Bibliography

Tocqueville, Alexis de. *Democracy in America*. New York: Alfred A. Knopf, 1954.

Tucker Benjamin. *Instead of a Book, By a Man Too Busy to Write One*. New York: Benj. R. Tucker, Publisher, 1897.

Turner, Frederick Jackson. *The Frontier in American History*. New York: Henry Holt & Company, 1920.

Warren, Josiah. *True Civilization*. Boston: J. Warren, 1863.

Woodcock, George. *Anarchism: A History of Libertarian Ideas and Movements*. Cleveland and New York: The World Publishing Company (Meridian Books), 1962.

INDEX